MW00711341

THE SPIRITUAL QUEST

CHRISTIAN SPIRITUAL DIRECTION IN 12 SIMPLE STEPS

Library of Congress Cataloging-in-Publication Data

Certain, Robert G., 1947-
  The spiritual quest : Christian spiritual direction in 12 simple steps / by Robert G. Certain.
        p.cm.
  Includes bibliographical references and index.
  ISBN (invalid) 978088201605 (pbk.)
  1. Spiritual direction--Christianity--Study and teaching. 2. Twelve-step programs--Religious aspects--Christianity. 3. Church group work. I. Title
  BV5053.C47 2008
  248.4--dc22
                                                          20007061812

Scripture quotations are from the *New English Bible*. Copyright © 1976 by Oxford University Press, Inc. © The Delegates of the Oxford University Press and the Syndics of the Cambridge University Press 1961, 1970. Used by permissio

THE SPIRITUAL QUEST

Copyright © 2008 by Robert G. Certain

All rights reserved.

No part of this book may be reproduced, stored in a retrieval system, or trans-mitted, in any form or by any means—electronic, mechanical, photocopying, recording or otherwise—without the prior written permission of the Author.

THE SPIRITUAL QUEST

The Spiritual Quest was developed in 1989 as part of a "Practicum in Spiritual Direction" under the oversight of the Reverend Dr. Robert D. Hughes of the School of Theology, Sewanee, Tennessee. It was designed for group spiritual direction in a parish setting. Because of the heightened awareness in society of unhealthy dependencies (alcohol, drugs, food, people), I chose to follow the Twelve Steps of Alcoholics Anonymous as a format for assisting people to recover from spiritual disease. The fourteen-week design includes one week of overview and introduction, one week on each of the Twelve Steps, and a concluding week.

The weekly seminars begin with worship (Eucharist or guided meditation), and include one hour of "Spiritual Friendship" sharing the prayer experience of the previous week, and one hour of lecture on the nature of one of the Steps. Once each month, the Spiritual Director (leader) meets with each participant for individual Direction. Following Step 5, the participants are *strongly encouraged* to make a private confession to a priest (not necessarily the Spiritual Director). The Director should provide participants with a list of area priests who are available to hear their confessions. It's also important that the Director be in spiritual direction, and have made a recent confession.

In addition to attending the weekly seminars, participants are expected to engage in servant ministry, to make a sacrificial pledge to the work of God's kingdom, to attend Lord's Day worship in their own church, and to read from the works of one or more Christian spiritual masters.

All of the materials used in the course are contained in this book so that the Spiritual Friends or Fellowship groups can pursue the Quest even in the absence of a person to present the Step materials. Persons planning to teach the course should become familiar with *The Twelve Steps and Twelve Traditions of Alcoholics Anonymous*, as well as various books on the practice of spiritual direction. It is expected that the course leader will develop his or her own presentation from this material. The material presented herein should be used in developing the leader's thoughts, but are not intended to be read word for word. Personal story is very important to model spiritual openness and intimacy.

Additional copies of this book as well as training seminars, other materials and tapes of presentations may be obtained from ETC Publications.

ETC Publications
Palm Springs, CA 92262

1-760-316-9695 Telephone
1-866-514-9969 Toll Free
1-760-316-9681 Fax

etc

etcpublications.com

E-mail : customer_service@etcpubliations.com

INDEX

INDEX

THE SPIRITUAL QUEST

A course of spiritual discipline, worship, study, friendship and direction

COURSE ELEMENTS

Weekly Seminars

Sharing with Spiritual Friend during Weekly Session

Daily Spiritual Discipline

> Morning or Evening Prayer and Bible Study
>
> Minimum of One Book Read from Bibliography
>
> Daily Journal (begun no later than Week 9)

Weekly Attendance at Sunday Eucharist

Private Confession (between Weeks 5 and 9)

Participation in Ministry of Outreach/Service (tithe of time)

Sacrificial Giving (tithe of treasure)

RECOMMENDED ADDITIONAL MATERIALS:

1979 *Book of Common Prayer*

Holy Bible, Modern Translation

Journal Book

12 STEPS of the Spiritual Quest

1. We admitted we were powerless over sin — that our lives had become unmanageable.

2. Came to believe that a Power greater than ourselves could restore us to sanity.

3. Made a decision to turn our will and our lives over to the care of God.

4. Made a searching and fearless moral inventory of ourselves.

5. Admitted to God, to ourselves, and to another human being the exact nature of our wrongs.

6. Were entirely ready to have God remove all these defects of character.

7. Humbly asked Him to remove our shortcomings.

8. Made a list of all persons we had harmed, and became willing to make amends to them all.

9. Made direct amends to such people wherever possible, except when to do so would injure them or others.

10. Continued to take personal inventory and when we were wrong promptly admitted it.

11. Sought through prayer and meditation to improve our conscious contact with God through Our Lord Jesus Christ, praying only for knowledge of His will for us and the power to carry that out.

12. Having had a spiritual awakening as the result of these steps, we tried to carry this message to others, and to practice these principles in our affairs.

TWELVE STEPS OF ALCOHOLICS ANONYMOUS

1. We admitted we were powerless over alcohol — that our lives had become unmanageable. 2. Came to believe that a Power greater than ourselves could restore us to sanity. 3. Made a decision to turn our will and our lives over to the care of God as we understood Him. 4. Made a searching and fearless moral inventory of ourselves. 5. Admitted to God, to ourselves, and to another human being the exact nature of our wrongs. 6. Were entirely ready to have God remove all these defects of character. 7. Humbly asked Him to remove our shortcomings. 8. Made a list of all persons we had harmed, and became willing to make amends to them all. 9. Made direct amends to such people wherever possible, except when doing so would injure them or others. 10. Continued to take personal inventory and when we were wrong promptly admitted it. 11. Sought through prayer and meditation to improve our conscious contact with God as we understood Him, praying only for knowledge of His will for us and the power to carry that out. 12. Having had a spiritual awakening as the result of these steps, we tried to carry this message to alcoholics, and to practice these principles in all our affairs.

The Twelve Steps are reprinted and adapted with permission of Alcoholics Anonymous World Services, Inc. Permission to reprint and adapt the Twelve Steps does not mean that AA has reviewed or approved the content of this publication, nor that the AA agrees with the views expressed herein. AA is a program of recovery from alcoholism — use of the Twelve Steps in connection with programs and activities which are patterned after AA, but which address other problems, does not imply otherwise.

THE SPIRITUAL QUEST
Landmarks on the Journey

Attendance		Worship	H.E.	Sun	Mon	Tue	Wed	Thu	Fri	Sat
Introduction	___	Week 1	___	___	___	___	___	___	___	___
Step 1	___	Week 2	___	___	___	___	___	___	___	___
Step 2	___	Week 3	___	___	___	___	___	___	___	___
Step 3	___	Week 4	___	___	___	___	___	___	___	___
Step 4	___	Week 5	___	___	___	___	___	___	___	___
Step 5	___	Week 6	___	___	___	___	___	___	___	___
Step 6	___	Week 7	___	___	___	___	___	___	___	___
Step 7	___	Week 8	___	___	___	___	___	___	___	___
Step 8	___	Week 9	___	___	___	___	___	___	___	___
Step 9	___	Week 10	___	___	___	___	___	___	___	___
Step 10	___	Week 11	___	___	___	___	___	___	___	___
Step 11	___	Week 12	___	___	___	___	___	___	___	___
Step 12	___	Week 13	___	___	___	___	___	___	___	___
Final	___	Week 14	___	___	___	___	___	___	___	___

Direction

Session 1 ___
Session 2 ___
Session 3 ___

Confession

Date _____

Book _____

Servant Ministry _____

Sacrificial Giving

A. Annual Income from all Sources $ _____

                                                          _____ x .10

B. Biblical Tithe $ _____

                                                          _____ - 52

C. Weekly Tithe $ _____

D. Current Weekly Gift to God $ _____

                                                          _____ x 52

E. Current Annual Gift to God $ _____

                                              + Line A _____

                                                          _____

                                                          _____ x 100

E. Current Percentage Gift to God   _____ %

If your current gift to God is less than a tithe, does it honestly represent a sacrificial gift to God for all the gifts He has given you? If not, decide what percentage of your income will (1) represent a sacrificial gift, (2) help you grow spiritually, and (3) move you toward the Biblical tithe. Then, fill out a new pledge card to your church and/or Christian charities to signify your commitment.

INTRODUCTION

The journey you are about to begin is called the *Spiritual Quest*. It is a simple, 12 Step guide to the not-so-simple task of being a disciple of Christ. In addition to the 12 Steps (modeled on the spiritual Steps of Alcoholics Anonymous), the Quest also involves daily prayer and Bible reading, reading from a Christian spiritual master, service ministry, sacrificial giving to the work of the Lord, the establishment of a Spiritual Friendship, consultation with a spiritual director, and regular participation in Lord's Day worship.

Spiritual Friendship

There are several concepts which require definition. One is *Spiritual Friendship*, which will be an integral part of the quest for a deeper relationship with the Lord. In a Spiritual Friendship two people are both giving and receiving guidance; they are acting as soul mates, or soul friends for each other. One hour each week will be an experience of Spiritual Friendship. Pick a person in your Quest group, do some initial conversation and exploration with different people for a week or two, and then settle on one person in the group with whom you will be sharing the fellowship hour at each session.

This relationship is egalitarian, an equal relationship. In order for it to be so, you have to exercise some discipline. Discipline is necessary to ensure that the time is evenly divided, according to the needs of the two people. It is really easy for a Spiritual Friendship to become one-sided, with one person listening and helping, and the other person doing all the talking. Avoid that; make yours a truly egalitarian relationship.

Spiritual Direction

The second term is *Spiritual Direction*. There's nothing equal about that relationship at all. Spiritual Direction is a relationship that is not symmetrical. In Spiritual Direction, the focus is on the directee's relationship with God, not the director's. In a direct session the concern will be your relationship with your Lord, and while the director may share his or her or her own story, that will not be the focus. The director will share only in order to help illuminate some things in your own life, and will try to assist you further on in your own pilgrimage. The director should also be in direction. You cannot drink of an empty well. So, he too must be going for direction.

Spiritual Direction focuses on the directee's personal relationship with God, as it is experienced by the directee. In other words, your experience is what you experience, there's nothing that we can add or detract from that. What we can do with your experience of God is to help understand it and help illuminate it. I can make it around my house with lights off, usually without killing myself, because I am familiar with what it looks like with the lights on, or in the daytime. I am less comfortable coming into the nave of the church to find the light switches. If I were to go into your house with the lights off and try to find my way around, I would probably kill myself—I would run into furniture or trip over stairs.

Many of us stay in the dark in our relationship with our Lord, and it's okay as far as it goes. You can make it around, you're familiar with your own prayer life, and perhaps you're fairly comfortable with it and confident you can get from point A to point B in your spiritual journey without a great deal of difficulty. Spiritual Direction is designed to illuminate that journey. So, like switching on a light in your room, you'll be able to see better, more clearly, and to move more directly into the relationship with your Lord.

Three Concerns

There are three concerns in Spiritual Direction. The first one is *you*; the second one is *your relationship with God*; and the third one is *God* himself: you, your relationship with God, and God. That seems simple enough, but so often when I listen to people, they focus only upon the relationship, and God gets lost. I hear others talking about a relationship with God, but their own person is missing. They say, "I'm not important, my life is unimportant. What the children are doing, or what my spouse is doing, or what the government is doing, that's not really important, it's just me and Jesus." Well, that is not healthy spiritually.

God made us and placed us in society. God thinks society is important; God thinks children, spouses, the government, and the economy are important. God thinks they are important, and God thinks you are important. You are not a drop in a puddle and maybe the drop that is making the mud moist at the bottom of the puddle.

Contemplating God is like getting to know a person for who he is. We can get to know other people pretty well without really establishing an intimate relationship with them. For instance, we can read pretty thorough biographies.

The focus of direction will be on the relationship. There is a rule in the Spiritual Relationship that anytime we get off track, we stop, we put the train back on the track, and get going again. So, if we start going off on a tangent in our conversation in the friendship sessions or in the direction session, then who-ever notices that the train is derailed and going off in some tangential direction, needs to say, "TIME-OUT, I think we're off track. Let's have three minutes of quiet, prayerful refocusing, and then let's try get back on course."

Direction vs. Therapy

In the book *Spiritual Friend*, by the Reverend Tilden Edwards, (an Episcopal priest at the Shalem Institute in Washington), there are a couple of pages where he describes the difference between psycho-therapy, pastoral counseling, and spiritual direction, and the purposes of the three of them. Therapy and counseling, for instance, are seeking solid self-definition—find out who you are; spiritual direction seeks knowing who we are, but then transcending that into a greater relationship, both with God and with God's people. Therapy and counseling on the one hand is concerned with the health of the individual, the integra-tion, social adjustment, the interior adjustment of the person; spiritual direction is concerned with filling the cup up to overflowing, filling us up with the love of Christ, so that it flows out and spills over on those around us, helping us to grow into the full stature of Christ.

Therapy and counseling are mind-talk; spiritual direction is God-talk: talking about the Lord, what the Lord is doing, and what we are doing in relationship with the Lord. Counseling and therapy generally have an end in mind, reintegration of the person, getting somebody up off their knees, and putting them back on their feet so that they can move out and function in society again, get over depression, or anxiety.

Spiritual direction can go on forever, because there's always more to a relationship than what we have experienced so far. That is true for our significant others, our spouses, our children, our parents, our siblings, and the people that we love the most. There's always more to them than we have experienced so far. These are finite human beings. With infinite God, too, there is always going to be more. So Spiritual Direction, the Spiritual Journey, the Spiritual Quest is an on-going process.

The Quest

I used the word "Quest" because it reminded me of Don Quixote. There's a wonderful phrase in the play "Man of LaMancha" where Don Quixote says, "The greatest madness of all is to accept the world as it is and not as it ought to be." In our Spiritual Growth, one of our focal points is to begin to see the world as it *ought to be*. We seek to view our Spiritual Friend, our families, and the people in our church and in our community as Christ-bearers. We seek to look through the masks and façades that we all put up around us to see the light of Christ that was placed there in our baptism — indeed, the light of God that was placed there in the creation. In the Quest, we seek to be able to see Christ's light and to act in relationship to that goodness that God placed there, to enable that goodness to grow and to bubble out to the surface, and to begin to displace the wickedness, the meanness, the brokenness, and the partiality that we are.

Confession

Another relationship that will be part of the Quest, and which is part of sound and significant spiritual growth is with a confessor. A confessor is one who hears auditory, private, sacramental confessions. There's a difference between confession and Spiritual Friendship or Spiritual Direction. In confession, the one who is making confession is obligated to tell it all, to be absolutely thorough and honest about all the things that are stirring around in our lives and eating our souls: the things we are ashamed of, the things that are painful, the things we wish we'd had never done, the things we regret not doing. The job of the confessor is to probe, like a surgeon, to help that venom, that spiritual cancer, come to the surface. Confession is pretty rigorous, but do not get anxious about it just yet. If you're not familiar with the practice of making a private confession; it will be explained in Steps 5, 6 and 7, and I will guarantee you it is a relief and not a burden.

In Spiritual Direction, the directee shares only what you want to share with the other person, and any questions or probes by either you or your Spiritual Friend or your Spiritual Director are gentle and can be turned aside. That is one of the rules in that relationship.

Confession is under the seal of the confessional. The secrecy of the confession is morally absolute for the person hearing the confession. Spiritual Direction and Friendship is confidential, which means you do not broadcast what you hear; you do not make it a topic of conversation under other circumstances; and you certainly do not add it to the gossip mill in the community. It does not necessarily mean that you go to the grave with it; and it does not mean you cannot bring up something in a later conversation with someone about how they're doing with it.

A lot of people confuse confidentiality with the seal of the confessional, and say, "I can't tell you that because it's confidential." Confidentiality requires a certain amount of judgment on your part as to what you are going to talk about with a third party. The rule is that you do not repeat outside the relationship anything you heard in confidence that you wouldn't be willing to repeat with that other person standing there with you.

Course Structure

While this is written to be a course of 14 weeks, the spiritual journey, growing in the Lord, lasts a life-time. The course design provides for a quarter-hour of guided meditation, an hour presentation by the Spiritual Director; and an hour of spiritual sharing with a friend—someone also in the group.

One hour each month participants are expected to make an appointment with the leader for spiritual direction. Sunday morning, or Lords Day worship is also expected. Regular group attendance is a course requirement. From time to time one or more members may, through no fault or design of their own be required to be away. If you discover that you have to be away, do three things—first, make sure that your spiritual friend knows you're not going to be here. If they do not know, and you are not here, we are going to wait and call you and try to find you, and we will worry about you if we do not know where you are. You are important to us.

The second thing to do is to make arrangements with your friend to meet for your hour together sometime during that week. Finally, arrange to pick up a copy of the lecture tape or read the material on the Step you missed, so you will not get behind the basis for your conversation with your spiritual friend during each weekly session, as well as for your daily spiritual discipline.

The daily spiritual discipline of Prayer Time is a pretty rudimentary one. It is basically "Daily Devotions for Individuals and Families" from the *Book of Common Prayer*. As you decide you want to expand your prayer time, then you can refer to the guide to the Daily Office provided at Step 11 to expand into more thorough use of the Prayer Book. (There was another group once upon a time, who used the Prayer Book like this, and they were forced out of the church for doing it. Because of their methodological use of the Prayer Book in their daily devotions, they were referred to as Methodists. So, this is dangerous stuff, to use the Prayer Book for daily devotions and worship.)

The next requirement is to read a minimum of one book from the Bibliography. If there is something else that you would rather read, check with the Director first. There are some authors that are not worth reading. Some writers will not qualify for this course. So, an approved book is part of the discipline.

Around Week 9, or earlier if you care to, begin keeping a daily journal to expand what you're doing in your prayer time.

Private confession to a priest will be explained and encouraged between Weeks 5 and 9. It is not necessarily the best thing for someone to have the same priest as director and confessor. The director will help you find a confessor.

The next course requirement is participation in ministry of outreach or service of some sort (a tithe of time). I'm not asking for 2.4 hours every day (a literal tithe of time), but it is important if you are going to grow spiritually to take the love of Christ beyond yourself. If you're not already engaged in some ministry of outreach or service, your director or pastor will help you find one that will fit your schedule. It doesn't have to be burdensome. You can have some fun with it and find it enjoyable.

Sacrificial giving (a tithe of treasure) is expected. The tithe (10% of income) is the Biblical standard. It is important that you be sacrificial. For somebody who's starting a car from a dead stop, a sacrifice would be almost anything. Make it a percentage; if you're not doing anything now, make it a half a percent. Don't say $2.00 or $10 or $20 or $50 a week, because that is not related to what you are receiving from God. Make it a proportionate gift, a percentage gift of what you are receiving. If you're giving a dollar amount now, convert that to percentage and go from there. Somebody once said, "Don't give 'til it hurts, give 'til it feels good."

There are some stages we go through in our giving back to God. One is guilt-giving when we give a little bit and feel guilty because we don't think it's enough. Another is grudge-giving where we are pushing ourselves toward a sacrifice, but we really don't like the discomfort of it very much. There is sacrificial giving, which pushes through the hurt phase and into the "Gosh, I just can't wait to give more" phase. In the Gospel, Jesus says "sell everything." I am not asking you to do that, and I am not asking you to go from zero to ten in a week. I'm asking you to search your own self, appraise your own person and your own obligations and your own resources, and what God has given you. Then make a sacrifice for the Lord. Sign a pledge form and turn it in as a way of sealing your commitment. That is a matter of spiritual growth, not church revenue. If you don't believe me, give your tithe directly to the diocese or to the President Bishop's Funds for World Relief. Keep it in the Christian church, if you will, but this is not for parish revenue purposes, this is for your spiritual growth.

Some Books

There are some books you will find useful: a 1979 Book of Common Prayer, a Bible—a modern translation that you will find to be helpful and beneficial as you read and understand. My personal favorite is the New English Bible, but the New International Version, the Jerusalem Bible, the Good News Bible, and a variety of other modern translations are very good. The Living Bible is a paraphrase so don't use it.

The bibliography is quite extensive and covers a number of centuries, going back to as early as the Church Fathers. But it is not exhaustive. Many are available in a good book store. The public library or a church library may have some.

If you have been reading a 20th century spiritual master, go for somebody in the Middle Ages or the Early Church. Broaden yourself. If you get into it 10 or 15 pages, and you decide you are not real crazy about it, do two things. First, read another 10 or 15 pages and see if it warms up to you. If it still doesn't, pick another one because there are hundreds of good things available.

The 12 Steps

This is not an AA or other recovery group meeting. Those of you who are familiar with AA or Al/Anon or Overeaters Anonymous or whatever, know that the 12 Steps say that we will "practice these principles in all our affairs," and your Christianity is one of your affairs. For those of you who have never been around a 12 Step recovery program, you may find it helpful to know that one of the founders of Alcoholics Anonymous was an Episcopal priest, and this is a very good staged way of developing your Christian spirituality. It's Step by Step and quite simple—not easy, but simple.

Step 1

The 1st Step is "We admitted that we were powerless over sin, and our lives have become unmanageable." As far as this course is concerned, we are really powerless over life—we are not the powers of life, God is. Life is not manageable by us. It is not meant to be managed. Life is intended by God to be lived and enjoyed, and God intends to be the One in charge. The admission that we really don't control our own lives is a difficult step to take, but it is absolutely and vitally important for all of us if we are going to grow in Christ.

Step 2

The 2nd Step is "Came to believe that a power greater than ourselves can restore us to sanity." That's how recovery groups talk about God. We talk about that power greater than ourselves as Christ Jesus, the Holy Trinity, God Almighty. During our sessions we'll talk about our Lord by whatever name we choose, because again, this is not a recovery meeting.

Step 3

Once we are convinced that God exists and can raise us up and place us where he wants us in this world, then the next thing on our part is the 3rd Step: "Made a decision to turn our wills and our lives over to the care of God as we understand him." That is all we can do. "God as we understand him" is all we can do, because we'll never understand all that there is to know about God. We hope that through Christian experience we will not understand God as a punishing God who is ready to beat us into a pulp if we ever make a decision to turn ourselves over to him.

Step 4

Once we've given ourselves over to the care of God, then we talk about searching our own interior lives, our own consciences, to discern what we have in stock. Moral inventory means to go in and take stock of everything: good, bad, and indifferent. Then you begin to sort it out and decide what can be discarded now, what can be kept as useful, what you might want to hold on to for a little while longer.

Step 5
After we have done that, then "We admit to God, to ourselves, and to another human being (preferably a priest of the church) the exact nature of our wrongs."

Steps 6 and 7
As we admit the nature of our wrongs, we "Become entirely ready to allow God to take them." It doesn't do us a whole lot of good to say, "This is my abiding sin, Lord, but I want to keep it." You need to be ready to say, "This is my abiding sin, Lord, and you can have it." Then ask him to forgive you. Once you're restored with God you begin a process of restoration with other people.

Steps 8 and 9
We make our list, we try to remember who it is we have offended, who it is we have hurt. We go to them whenever possible, except if doing so would injure them or cause trouble for that person. We don't cause more trouble in the process of clearing our own consciences. We hold on to our bad conscience in order to do a good turn for somebody else.

Step 10
Then we begin life anew by trying to live constantly asking ourselves how would Christ act? What is my responsibility as a Christian person? Have I done wrong? Have I done right? That's what we mean by continuing to take personal inventory. When we goof up, we admit it. It doesn't hurt to admit it. The reason Richard Nixon was driven out of office was because he lied, not because he ordered the break-in of Watergate. If he had said, "Heck, yeah, George McGovern was a commie, pinko spy and I broke in there. It was national security. I'm glad I did it, and I'd do it again tomorrow." Everybody would have said, "Richard Nixon is a little screwy, but he is still the President." But he lied about it, so he got kicked out of office. So, admitting our wrongs, quickly, is the very best thing we can do. But we can't do that at the beginning of the journey, because we have to build up courage and trust God first.

Step 11
Continuing through our prayer life beyond this stage, we seek God's will in our lives. Instead of praying AT a situation, we pray FOR it. Instead of saying, "Lord, make my boss understand my situation and give me a raise, or a better desk," we say, "Lord, I don't understand exactly what's going on in everybody's lives in that office and the corporation, but may your will be done and let me understand your will and seek to do it." That's praying <u>for</u> a situation rather than *at* it. Did you ever get the feeling when somebody says, "I'm praying for you" that you'd really rather they wouldn't? Well, I do when I think that people are praying at me; they really want me to change, and they're asking God, "Change that man." "Let the Lord's will be done in someone's life" is a more appropriate focus for prayer.

Step 12
The 12th Step is to share the Gospel, to share the good news of God in Jesus Christ in our own lives with those around us, and to be a Christian in all our affairs whether we are at church or whether we are down at the business or whether we're in the house, or on a journey or whatever we are doing. We are to be more than Sunday Christians, more than private Christians. We are to be public Christians, too.

Getting Started

That then, is the Spiritual Quest. If you wish to journey further, start looking for a spiritual friend to go with you. Look over the Bibliography in the back of this book and start checking out something of interest. Then turn to the following pages entitled "Keys to Effective Prayer" and try out the suggestions you find there. More help with prayer will be given as you progress in the Quest, or you may seek help from someone whose prayer skills are more mature than your own.

KEYS to EFFECTIVE PRAYER

PRAYER PLACES

Some places that modern Christians have found suitable for private prayer are:

The back of a church or chapel

Your own bedroom

A little-used room in your home

A secluded spot outdoors

The important thing about a prayer place is that it helps us to pray better. Picking the right place is one of the keys to effective prayer.

PRAYER TIMES

Unless there is a commitment to fixed times, there is not likely to be much prayer. That's just the way we human beings are made. Four popular times for prayer that people have tried and found helpful are:

After rising and showering in the morning

During the noon lunch break

After returning from work, before supper

Immediately before retiring

Finding the right schedule for daily prayer is going to take experimentation and dedication. Getting a schedule that fits your life-style may take months, but it is worth the effort. Prayer is that important.

PRAYER POSTURE

Posture also plays a key role in the way we pray. Just as you can pray anywhere and anytime, so you can pray in any posture. The best posture is the one that helps you to pray. Here are some recommended positions:

Lie on your bed or the floor, legs flat, heels together, and eyes fixed on the ceiling

Sit erect in a chair, both feet flat on the floor, hands in your lap or resting palms down on the arms of the chair

Kneel upright at your bed, back straight, hands resting on the bed for support.

Sit on the floor, legs crossed and pulled in toward the body, back straight and pressed against the wall, hands in lap or on knees with palms open up or down.

Excerpted from *YOU: Prayer for Beginners and Those Who Have Forgotten How*, by Mark Link, S.J. © 1976

PRAYER MOOD

After choosing a place, time, and posture, the next step is to create a mental climate for prayer. Some methods that people have found helpful are the following:

BREATHING

Take the position you intend to use in prayer. Next, relax your body. Begin with the muscles of your face and move down through your shoulders, chest, arms, and legs. Now, observe your breathing. Close your eyes and try to establish a pattern of slow, deep, even breathing. Continue this until a mood of concentration sets in.

LISTENING

Close your eyes and listen to the sounds around you. Let them penetrate your being—freely and deeply. Continue this until a mood of quiet sets in.

HEARTBEAT

Close your eyes and listen to your heartbeat. When you become aware of it, monitor its rhythm. Monitor it until a mood of interior focus begins.

SENSATION

Become aware of your clothes gripping your shoulders, legs, arms; your shoes gripping your feet; the chair gripping your body. Monitor these sensations until relaxation sets in. As with other aspects of the prayer process, creating the "mood" for prayer will vary from person to person. Trial and error is the only way to discover what works best for you.

PRESENCE OF GOD

After the place, time, posture, and mood have been taken care of, you are ready for the key Step in the prayer process: opening yourself to God's presence.

Here are some prayers, asking God to help you to open yourself to His presence. Each fits with one of the four mood-building exercises: breathing, listening, heartbeat, sensation. After each exercise, pray slowly and reflectively the appropriate prayer:

[breathing]
"Father,
You are closer to me
than my own breath.
May each breath I take
deepen my awareness of Your presence."

[listening]
"Father,
You are as real
as the sounds around me.
May each sound I hear
deepen my awareness of Your reality."

[heartbeat]
"Father,
You are as present and life-giving
as my own heart.
May each heartbeat I experience
deepen my awareness of Your presence."

[sensation]
"Father,
You embrace me as certainly
as the clothes I wear.
May each sensation I feel
deepen my awareness of Your loving embrace."

After having prayed one of the above prayers, pause in the posture of openness to God's presence. If God makes His presence felt, as he does from time to time, stay with it as long as it engages you prayerfully.

STEP 1:

Admitted that we were powerless over sin and that our lives had become unmanageable.

In Luke 14:25-33, we get a little bit of a story that helps us to recall that and makes the point of Step 1:

"Great multitudes accompanied Jesus and he turned and he said to them 'If anyone comes to me and does not hate his own father and mother and wife and children and brothers and sisters, yes and even his own life he cannot be my disciple. Whoever does not bear his own cross and come after me cannot be my disciple. For which of you desiring to build a tower does not first sit down and count the cost whether he has enough to complete it? Otherwise, when he has laid the foundation and is not able to finish it, all who see it begin to mock him, saying "This man began to build and was not able to finish." Or what king going to encounter another king in war will not sit down first and take counsel whether he is able with 10,000 to beat him who comes against him with 20,000. And if not, while the other is yet a great way off, he sends an embassy and asks terms of peace. So therefore, whoever of you does not renounce all that he has cannot be my disciple.'"

Jesus reminds us to take stock of exactly what our personal abilities are without the help of the Lord. To do so is to admit that we're not in control. One of the most freeing things in the world is to be not in control, to acknowledge that while there is much that I can do alone, there is much, much more that I can do with God.

Bishop John MacNaughton of the Episcopal Diocese of West Texas wrote a stewardship book some time ago in which he quoted an agricultural study done at Iowa State University concerning what it took to produce corn from an acre of land. It went through all the nutrients, the rain, and the sunshine that were necessary, and determined that the farmer's labor accounted for only 5% of the requirements to produce a bushel of corn. Everything else was already in the earth, created by God, or given by God in the form of rain at the right time during the growing season. As hard as a farmer works, and I'll grant you that it is hard work, 5% is all they can claim. Bishop MacNaughton's point in relating the report is that we are the receivers of gifts, and that we are not in control of those gifts. God is in control of them. The admission that we have power over nothing is the first step in spiritual liberation.

Humility

One word that is used for this 1st Step in spiritual growth is "humility." Humility gives us the ability to recognize that we are the servants of God and not the masters of God, and to be able to swallow our own personal pride and say "There is a better way of doing something." Perhaps the person who comes up with the better way is a 5 year-old child, or a junior employee, or maybe the next door neighbor who has been a thorn in your flesh for ten years, or some other person that you would never think of as having any great insight.

The things that block our avenue to God become to be our obsessions and our attachments. No one can follow Christ unless he first renounces the obsession, the attachment to everything else: father, mother, lands, children, crops, flocks. As long as we hold on to them we close Christ out of our life. When we find ourselves saying "I have to fix this situation" then there is a pretty good chance that we have become overly attached. Step 1 in spiritual growth is acknowledging that we are not in charge. Part of what we people, particularly we Americans, use as a gauge of who we are, is our position in society, the amount of possessions we have, the amount of influence we exert, and who our friends and our families are. The more important those things are to us, the more we try to keep them good and perfect, to mold them, to shape them, to influence them, and to build them. The richer a person becomes, the more interested he gets in the stock market. The person with no money could care less what the stock market does. Possessions have a way of beginning to take control of us. We think we control them but they claim our time, thoughts, and energy to maintain them.

Renouncing Our Idols

Renouncing things, turning our back on our idolatrous possessions is what this step is all about. All people place great reliance on our ability to do things, to accomplish something, to build, or on our intelligence, our good taste, or our good looks, or whatever it is that drives us and gives us identity. What Jesus is saying in Luke is that in fact, what we have, what we do, what we count on, is not all that reliable, that we are indeed powerless somewhere, even in all of our apparent power.

During the height of the cold war, we had enough weaponry in this country to destroy the world several times over. We were held hostage by our own destructive ability. We were powerless <u>not</u> to use it. We were powerless <u>to</u> use it. If we used our nuclear forces, we would destroy ourselves and the rest of the world in the process. If we chose to eliminate our arsenals, we laid ourselves and our allies open to aggressions. Our destructive ability failed as a resource to negotiate terms of disarmament and peace in the world. In the middle of 1989 the economy of Eastern Europe finally broke the stalemate. They could no longer afford to pour millions and billions of dollars into arms because they were running out of food and housing and, in order to prevent a revolution, war-making had to be put on the back burner. So, all the power of the Soviet Union was no good.

When the students of Iran took over the American Embassy in 1979, the United States was powerless to do anything about it. President Carter tried to do something, but failed. Airplanes ran into one another and part of the rescue force wound up getting killed and the rest had to be plucked out of the desert of Iran.

In Vietnam, we were powerless to bring the war to a conclusion, even though we had more power, more bombs, more guns, more ammunition, and more sophistication than the North Vietnamese regulars and the South Vietnamese insurgents. Power—our abilities, our accomplishments, our possessions—no matter how much we have, is limited and ultimately useless to us. In the 14th chapter of Luke, Jesus is calling us to take stock of that and be honest about it. He says "If you think you're invulnerable, you better sit down and re-evaluate your position."

Don't forget certain stories from the Old Testament, like Gideon, when you're outmanned. When the enemy had the advantage 4 to 1, they were still defeated, not because Gideon had a bigger army, but because God did it. When Joshua fought the battle of Jericho, the Israelites didn't fire a shot. They just scared the dickens out of the people in Jericho and the people in Jericho killed each other. It was God's power that brought it about.

Our Worth Is in God

This Step is not saying that you're worthless. Instead spiritual growth helps us to discover the vast worth that we have in the sight of God. But it is not worth based upon what we do, what we own, what we control in this world. It is worth based upon the light of Christ that was placed there in our baptisms and on the image of God that was placed there in our creation. That is where the worth is to be found and that is the background for Step 1. The admission that we own, control, and have power over nothing is the 1st Step in spiritual growth.

Perhaps God intended control over the earth to be our possession in the beginning, but Adam and Eve had that unfortunate little incident in the third chapter of Genesis that stopped all that right off before there were more than two people on the face of the earth. You remember the story of the fall, which begins in the third chapter of Genesis.

> "Now the serpent was more subtle than any other wild creature that the Lord had made. He said to the woman, 'Did God say you shall not eat of any tree in the garden?' And the woman said to the serpent, 'We may eat of the fruit of the trees of the garden. But God said "You shall not eat of the fruit of the tree which is in the midst of the garden, neither shall you touch it, lest you die."' But the serpent said to the woman, 'You will not die. For God knows that when you eat of it your eyes will be opened and you will be like God, knowing good and evil.' So when the woman saw that the tree was good for food and that it was a delight to the eyes, and that the tree was to be desired to make one wise, she took of its fruit and ate. And she also gave some to her husband and he ate. Then the eyes of both were opened and they knew that they were naked, and they sewed fig leaves together and made themselves aprons."

It is a tragic story because when God created man, "male and female he created them, in the likeness and image of God he created them." We were already in the image of God. And the serpent, the seducer, said, "No, no, no. What will make you like God is not what God has done, but what you can do." The seduction was set; and the seduction has been set with every generation since then. We are fools for it, to believe that we have the power to become like God on our own, by something we do, when the creation story says we are already there. And when we grasp that which God would give us, when we take it by force, we lose it.

So God, in order to protect us human beings, drove us out of the Garden of Eden. It was not so much punishment. Remember there was another tree in the Garden that had also been forbidden—the tree of eternal life. It would have been a terrible, terrible punishment to live forever as moral beings subject to sin and alienation.

There is a joke told about a doctor who died and went to heaven. When he arrives before the Pearly Gates, there is a long line. He walks on by it and up to St. Peter. "I'm Dr. Smith," he says. Peter says, "The line forms at the rear." Dr. Smith says, "Didn't you hear me? I'm a *doctor*." St. Peter says, "I know. The line forms at the rear." So he goes on back and more people come up behind him and in a few minutes here comes a man in a white coat and a stethoscope, and he just trots right on past the gate. St. Peter's up there checking off names and this guy in the white coat comes by, and St. Peter just waves at him, and in he goes. And Dr. Smith was incensed at that. He walked up to St. Peter and said, "Hey, what's the deal here?" Peter said "What do you mean, what's the deal?" He said, "You wouldn't let me in. I'm a doctor, and I saved a lot of lives, and you wouldn't let me come into heaven. You said I had to wait in line." "Yeah, that's right, that's the rule." "Well, what about that other doctor that came by?" He said, "What other doctor?" "The guy in the white coat that came by here just a minute ago. St. Peter said, "Oh, that wasn't a doctor. That was God. He just likes to dress up and play doctor every once in a while."

Renouncing Our Power Unleashes God's Power

That's what we like to do, dress up and play God every once in a while. That is no way to be. Adam and Eve weren't the only people to have the problem, and it didn't stop sometime in the Davidic kingdom. Paul had been one of the best people in the whole nation about being perfect, being in control, the Pharisee's Pharisee. He grew up in a rich family in Tarsus, a Roman citizen, wealthy enough to study at the feet of Gamaliel, the high priest, and to know the Torah, keep kosher, and live an exemplary Jewish life. This is what he says about all that in his letter to the Romans (7:14ff):

"We know that the law is spiritual; but I am not: I am unspiritual, the purchased slave of sin. I do not even acknowledge my own actions as mine, for what I do is not what I want to do, but what I detest. But if what I do is against my will, it means that I agree with the law and hold it to be admirable. But as things are, it is no longer I who perform the action, but sin that lodges in me. For I know that nothing good lodges in me—in my unspiritual nature, I mean— for though the will to do good is there, the deed is not. The good which I want to do, I fail to do; but what I do is the wrong which is against my will; and if what I do is against my will, clearly it is no longer I who am the agent, but sin that has its lodging in me.

"I discover this principle, then: that when I want to do the right, only the wrong is within my reach. In my inmost self I delight in the law of God, but I perceive that there is in my bodily members a different law, fighting against the law that my reason approves and making me a prisoner under the law that is in my members, the law of sin. Miserable creature that I am, who is there to rescue me out of this body doomed to death? God alone, through Jesus Christ our Lord! Thanks be to God! In a word then, I myself, subject to God's law as a rational being, am yet, in my unspiritual nature, a slave to the law of sin.

"The conclusion of the matter is this: there is no condemnation for those who are united with Christ Jesus, because in Christ Jesus the life-giving law of the Spirit has set you free from the law of sin and death. What the law could never do, because our lower nature robbed it of all potency, God has done."

In other words, Paul recognized that he was powerless over sin, that his attempts to control it in his life were insane, and that there was one who could restore him to sanity, and that one was Christ.

The self-affirmation movement of the last few decades, and the so-called "New Age" movement, is a search for self-confidence built on the quicksand of suppressed sin. My hunch is that there is a considerable sense of worthlessness in people, a sense that may not even find good articulation. Instead of filling that sense of worthlessness with the worth of Jesus in our lives, it is being filled with self. It by-passes the Christian Gospel in search of something else, but which cannot fill the need.

In part, this situation is the Church's fault, because the Church is responsible for much guilt in our culture, and for giving its blessing to a lot of evil in the world, and for saying good is evil and evil is good. In part, it is an abandonment of the faith of the generations, the tradition of Jews and Christians back to Abraham and beyond that is the real source of solid rock on which faith can be built. There are many books on the market today that promote a self-actualization that builds personal worth upon no foundation. It would be like building a 12- or 14-story condominium on a coastal island or beach without piers or foundations under it. It looks good for a while, and it will stand up under some light winds and low surf; but in a hurricane, the sand underneath is going to wash away and the whole thing will collapse.

A Foundation for Faith

The Spiritual Quest is a re-examination of foundational Christian faith. It will go behind and beyond things like the *Book of Common Prayer*, or stained glass windows, our degrees from college or our successes, or whatever else that we build our faith on.

God loves us, not because of what we accomplish, but because of who we are—his creation. He has given each of us various talents and gifts. What we do with it is a measure of our response to God, but it is not a measure of our own worth before God. There is not one of us in this room who can turn the light switch on or off by ourselves. You just can't do it. You don't work the power station. You didn't make the plastic; you didn't pump the oil that went into the plastic; you didn't run the wires, you didn't build the building yourself; and you didn't connect it up to the power station. It takes all that support to turn on a simple light switch. It really is not a bad thing to say, "I'm really connected to hundreds of people all over the world." We are a people created to live in community; but it takes some humility to acknowledge that we are not the axis around which that community and the rest of the universe rotate. Humility is not one of our favorite virtues, but it is necessary if we are to successfully accomplish Step 1 and surrender to our lack of power over sin.

Surrender Is Not All Bad

The very idea of surrender presents most people with a great obstacle; but my experience tells me that surrender is not all bad—in fact it can be the only course that leads to life. When I was shot down over North Vietnam in 1972, I landed near an agricultural community northwest of Hanoi. I was immediately surrounded by over fifty Vietnamese, some with automatic rifles. The only possibility I had to survive the night was to throw down my own weapon and to surrender. As a result, I lived through the prison experience and eventually found new freedom and life back home in the United States.

Another surrender was less dramatic, but by far more important to my spiritual growth. When I was fifteen years old, I first came to believe that God was calling me to ordained ministry. For the next ten years I did everything I could think of to "do it my way" and to follow my own course. While I loved flying for the Air Force, was very good at it, and my war record would have opened my career up to great things in aviation, I had to finally surrender to God's call to ministry in order to have a fulfilled life and not just an exciting one. Had I not gone to seminary, I might have had a distinguished military career, but I would have died spiritually. By surrendering to God, I have had a fulfilling ministry, a distinguished career as a reserve Chaplain, and I can still fly airplanes.

Humble admission of powerlessness over sin and life does not close us off from our fulfillment as people, it opens us up to that fulfillment and serves as the foundation upon which God will help us build our futures.

To step into the opening provided by Christ, begin a regular, daily time of prayer and Bible study. Follow the guide on the next page as a discipline for this week.

SPIRITUAL FRIENDSHIP

Choose someone to explore Friendship.

        Share your experience of prayer during the past week.

        What have you learned about your own lack of power to manage life?

        What are your hopes and fears about the 12 Steps?

        Have you selected a servant ministry? What is it? Have you begun?

PRAYER TIME - STEP 1
Theme: Human Weakness

Step 1: Admitted we were powerless over sin and that our lives are unmanageable.

Format
> Preparation (breath prayer, relaxation exercise, etc)
> Read Psalm
> Silence (5 minutes)
> Read Scripture selection
> Silence (5 minutes)
> Personal prayers
> Lord's Prayer
> Collect of the week

Day 1:	Psalm 10	Micah 7:1-6
2:	14	Revelation 3:17-19
3:	22	Romans 7:14-24
4:	37:1-18	Matthew 26:36-39
5:	38	Matthew 7:3-5
6:	42	Romans 5:6-11
7:	44	Isaiah 35:3-4

Collect

O God, the strength of all who put their trust in you: Mercifully accept our prayers; and because in our weakness we can do nothing good without you, give us the help of your grace, that in keeping your commandments we may please you both in will and deed; through Jesus Christ our Lord, who lives and reigns with you and the Holy Spirit, one God, for ever and ever. Amen.

Sixth Sunday after the Epiphany (Book of Common Prayer, p. 216)

STEP 2
Came to believe that a power greater than ourselves could restore us to sanity.

Once we have admitted that we were powerless over sin, and that our lives are unmanageable, it is a very short step to recognize that we are just a little bit insane. Now, there are a lot of people who think that insanity is a real stigma. However, those of us who have been there and have returned in some measure, find that there is a new appreciation for life that comes as a result of recognizing that understanding of the world was a little bit distorted. Insanity, in part, is not recognizing real reality; it is having a reality that is different from others. It can take the form of grandiose thinking, thinking we are super people and God's gift to humanity. It can take the form of self-loathing, thinking that we are worthless in the eyes of God and humanity. It is also doing the same thing in the same way over and over, expecting different results. Insanity is irrational and distorted thinking or perception.

It Began with the Fall

Part of the background of "coming to believe that a power greater than ourselves can restore us to sanity" goes all the way back to the Fall. It was crazy of Adam and Eve to think that by eating of the fruit of the tree of the knowledge of good and evil they could become like God; it was crazy because they were already like God. God had accomplished that in creation. On the sixth day "God created man in his own image; in the image of God he created him; male and female he created them." Eating some fruit to change into that likeness was insane. It is also called original sin.

Who is Jesus for You?

All of us have been taught something about Jesus. You have heard a lot of images and titles and stories about him, in the Scripture and in the tradition, in the stories you heard at your mama's knee, in the stories you heard in Sunday School, and in your own story, your own experience of God in your life. A lot of images, titles, names, analogies, and functions come to mind: King of Kings, Father, Story Teller, Miraculously Conceived, Judge, Friend, Teacher, Healer, Creator, Miracle Worker, Son, Holy Spirit, and so forth. Many of them are clearly scriptural; some derive from an experience we have had.

The main picture that we see from the titles for God is one that I think is inherently and patently true in the Gospels, in Paul's writings, and in the other epistles and writings of the New Testament. Jesus is always pictured by the Gospel writers and by Paul as our friend; Jesus has good will towards us. He heals the sick, casts out demons, restores broken relationships, raises the dead to life, heals the community, brings the community back together. The New Testament is full of those kinds of stories.

The woman caught in adultery is not condemned by our Lord, she is saved by Him, not just in terms of salvation for the Kingdom of God, but she is saved from the mob, which had every legal right to stone her. Stoning somebody did not mean hitting them a couple of times with a rock. It meant throwing stones at them until their bodies were covered up completely by a pile of stones. If wounding did not kill them, the weight of the stones and the suffocation that would follow being covered over with piles of stones would. Jewish law provided for that punishment for women who were caught in adultery. Nevertheless, Jesus did not condemn her. He did not condemn the publican who comes in and lays his offerings down and never raises his head, but asks for God's mercy; rather, He points to him, as somebody who really knows where he stands in relation with God: unworthy and in need of God's love, mercy, and forgiveness.

When Lazarus, who was one of Jesus' close friends and the brother of Mary and Martha, dies, He raises him from the dead. He doesn't say, "Gosh, it's too bad, I was running a little late; I didn't think he was that sick." When the centurion asked for healing for his servant, Jesus doesn't say, "Don't bother me, boy;" He heals him. When the woman touches the hem of His garment, He didn't do anything, but she was healed and He felt the power coming out. When He asked the disciples, "Who was it that brushed up against me?" They laughed and said, "What are you talking about? We're in the midst of the market place! Come on, Jesus, there are hundreds of people around here, it could have been anybody." So, our Lord heals, He responds to the demoniac, restores him to his right mind; He heals the epileptic boy by driving the demon of epilepsy out, and so on.

Good News!

Jesus, being God's incarnate, is the perfect picture of God's coming to us to love us. There is no difference between the Father's attitude towards us and the Son's. The Son embodies the Father's attitude; He enfleshes it and makes it so that we can see it and touch it and feel it in this life.

However, many people are afraid of God. They don't even want to have anything to do with God or religion or anything like that, because what has been transmitted in our culture as God is something totally at odds with Christianity, but which is promulgated by people who claim Christ as their Lord and Savior. That is, God the Father would really like nothing better than to send every one of you to hell in a hand basket. He has a small little place called heaven that has room for 144,000 people from each of the 12 tribes of Israel. Of course, if anybody reads Revelation, they know the next verse says, "I looked and saw a vast throng, which no one could count, from every nation, of all tribes, peoples, and languages, standing in front of the throne and before the Lamb." But people who want to narrow God down to having a little box with just room for 144,000 don't read that next verse.

The difficulty that we 21st Century Americans have so very much of the time, is that the common image of God is of a bad guy, a really angry old father who is crotchety in his old age, and who would really just as soon bring another flood, but has decided that a few can be saved. So He is going to let Jesus come down and give everybody a perfect example. Anybody who can follow the perfect example can be saved. Anybody who cannot, gets to burn. The Father gets to send them off to hell for the Angel of Light (Lucifer) to deal with. That image is wrong, just plain wrong. God is always working for the restoration of the relationship between humanity and God, and that is true everywhere in scripture.

Jesus is not some kind of cosmic narrow way that only skinny people can get through to. Jesus opens up a way for all of us, becomes a bridge builder. Jesus is our friend. He tells stories designed to turn people's thinking upside down so that they can realize the truth that was around them, the truth that God loves them and that God works in our behalf in all kinds of strange ways that we would never anticipate.

The story of the Good Samaritan is an upsetting story to a First Century Hebrew. Jesus teases them, when the man who was making a trip is lying there on the side of the road. Of course, that was no surprise because everybody would have been watching and waiting for the thugs to jump out. It's kind of like when I went to see *Platoon* with 180 Vietnam veterans. In the scene where they're walking through the jungle, you could feel the tension in the men in that room because it was the kind of place where ambushes occurred, and people started shouting at the people on the screen, "Look out!" So that is the kind of scene that Jesus builds with that story. Then sure enough, the poor guy gets mugged and he is left there half dead. Then the heroes start coming in. The priest is a hero; the Levite is a hero. Then, here comes that scoundrel Samaritan who is likely to do the guy in. The people would expect that this fellow is going to add insult to injury by killing him and stealing anything left. But in fact Jesus turns the story upside down, and the hated enemy, the illegitimate cousin of the Jewish people, the Samaritan, saves the man, rescues him, uses his own resources to heal him. He administers first aid by washing his wounds and pouring on wine. The alcohol would act as an astringent to clean out the wound. He then took him to a place where he could be cared for properly. He didn't care who he was, or what his circumstances were. So that turns the thinking upside down.

A similar story in my life was that the people who saved my life in the countryside of North Vietnam were the soldiers with the guns. They rescued me and saved me. It was not the F-4s and the helicopters from the American side; it was the Vietnamese soldiers with the guns who kept me safe from the civilians who really seemed to be planning some other end for me. So the hated enemy is the rescuer. Jesus says that this is how we are restored; we are restored in all kinds of ways. God even uses our enemies to administer his grace to us. And He is always working to administer grace.

The idea that there are just a few who are the elect for whom Jesus died is not scriptural. If you are going to narrow the elect down to a few people who get saved, and then get to sit back and gloat at all those poor sinners out there who are going to hell, then you have missed the point. The way Jesus tells the story is that anybody who starts gloating is well on the way to hell already. Harlots, prostitutes, tax-gatherers are going to come into the Kingdom of God before the presumed elect. He made the Pharisees mad when He said that; but that is what He said. God is not going to send the Pharisees to hell, that is not the point. The people who are broken, the people who recognize that they indeed cannot earn salvation, indeed have not done anything, have not done God any favors, and who recognize their estrangement from God and their continuing need to have more and more of our persons converted to Christ, are the ones who will find that conversion happening. If you are perfect, you don't need to change any more, right? So, all those who think they are perfect have cut themselves off from further grace.

God is for Us! Who is to Condemn?

So, the first thing we have to do here is to step back from perverse images of Jesus, perverse images of God the Father, that suggest God is against us and working for bad things. Such perverse images are often accompanied by the phrase, "It was God's will."

Whenever I have to bury children, teenagers, or young adults, it really boils my blood for somebody to say "It was God's will." I consider that blasphemy. I don't believe God visits punishment and suffering on children. When I came home from Vietnam and people said it was God's will that I lived, I resisted that judgment, too, because of the implication of the other side. I was not the only person on my airplane. There were six people on the crew, and only three of us came home. I cannot believe that it was God's will that Don Rissi, Bobby Thomas and Walter Ferguson died that night. So I have to reject the whole package.

It is God's will that I live as fully and completely as possible in accordance with His will in the time that I have. I think it is God's will that I do what I can to live a little additional life, a little bit more than others, to live something of the life of those friends of mine who died in Vietnam. Insurance companies do not call "Acts of God" such things as sunshine, pretty days, and the fact that houses don't burn down; insurance companies call volcanoes, earthquakes, tornadoes, hurricanes, and lightening strikes "Acts of God." Those are acts of nature, of God's created order, yes. Some of them are acts of human beings, also part of God's created order. They are not acts of God, but are part of what is still not complete about creation. God creates by bringing order out of chaos. God comes to us as the One who is going to bring order out of our chaos, who restores us to fellowship with Himself, restores us to fellowship with other people, who builds up our community. God is the One who is working to heal our sickness, to eliminate cancer, strokes, horrible catastrophes, Parkinson's disease, genetic disorders, the death of innocents, grudge-holding and hatred and wars. God is trying to do away with all that is evil and destructive.

Restoration of Sanity

Step 2 has to do with the restoration of sanity. We have a wonderful story in the synoptic Gospels that makes the point. The account in Mark's Gospel is the first half of the fifth chapter:

"They (the apostles and Jesus) came to the other side of the sea of Galilee to the country of the Gerasenes, (the eastern shore of Galilee), and when he (Jesus) had come out of the boat, there met them out of the tombs a man with an unclean spirit who lived among the tombs; and no one could bind him any more, even with a chain, for he had often been bound with fetters and chains, but the chains he wrenched apart and the fetters he broke in pieces. No one had the strength to subdue him. Night and day among the tombs and on the mountains, he was always crying out and bruising himself with stones. And when he saw Jesus from afar he ran and worshiped him, and crying out with a loud voice said, 'What have you to do with me, Jesus, Son of the most high God? I adjure you by God do not torment me,' for he had said to them, 'Come out of the man, you unclean spirit.' And Jesus asked him, 'What is your name?' He replied, 'My name is Legion for we are many,' and he begged him eagerly not to send them out of the country. Now a great herd of swine was feeding there on the hillside, and they begged him, 'Send us into the swine, let us enter them.' So he gave them leave, and the unclean spirits came out and entered the swine and the herd, numbering about two thousand, rushed down the steep bank into the sea and were drowned in the sea. The herdsman fled and told it in the city and in the country. People came to see what had happened and they came to Jesus and saw the demoniac sitting there, clothed, and in his right mind—the man who had had the legion—and they were afraid, and those who had seen it told what had happened to the demoniac and to the swine. And they began to beg Jesus to depart from their neighborhood. And as he was getting into the boat, the man who had been possessed by demons begged that he might go with him. But he refused and said to him, 'Go home to your friends, tell them how much the Lord has done for you, and how he has had mercy on you.'"

That story is familiar to us; it is a wonderful story. The guy was crazy as a June bug. Jesus comes in and says, "Get out of there." The swine career into the Sea of Galilee and drown. Then the man is just sitting there, normal.

Partners with God

We cannot do it without God. And God will not do it without us. God calls us to partnership to work with Him; He restores us in order that we may work together. My argument here in Step 2 is that God's purpose towards us humans is now, and always has been, friendly. God is not the bad guy in this deal. Our fathers, our earthly fathers, may have been real jerks, they may have been real saints, but they are not God. God is the perfect one; the one who loves us to distraction, loves us enough to become one of us, and to submit to whatever we would do with it.

When the word "judge" is used, we have to remember that a judge is somebody who tells the truth, who discerns the truth and speaks it. A judge is not somebody who sends somebody off to the gas chamber, necessarily. A judge discerns the truth, and the truth is in Christ Jesus. As we dwell in Christ Jesus there is life in us—THAT is true. The truth about us as baptized Christians is that Christ dwells within us. The truth that the judge is going to see is that we are the redeemed, the beloved children of God.

The Beloved of God

In your breath prayer this week say, "I am the beloved of God." If in searching your own heart you don't believe that, use the prayer as your mantra until you do. When you are walking down the street and not using your brain for anything else, use it as a mantra. God can make you whole and give you life abundant, that is what Jesus said He came to bring.

I urge you in your prayers this week to consider very carefully that God's love is for you in all its perfection, and that God is working through Christ to restore you to the glory that was in the beginning. You may not make it in this life, but that is what God is working for.

SPIRITUAL FRIENDSHIP
STEP 2: Came to believe that a Power greater than ourselves could restore us to sanity.

Choose a partner with whom you would like to share for the remainder of the quarter.

Discussion Topics
Share your experience of prayer time during the past week.
How have you been aware of Jesus' presence in your life this past week?
What thought, belief, or behavior patterns of yours would you characterize as "insane"?
Do you really want relief from them?
Do you believe, at least intellectually, that Jesus wants you to change?
Do you make a sacrificial pledge to the work of Christ?

PRAYER TIME - STEP 2
Theme: God's Power

STEP 2: Came to believe that a power greater than ourselves could restore us to sanity.

Format
    Preparation (breath prayer, relaxation exercise, etc)
    Read Psalm
    Silence (5 minutes)
    Read Scripture selection
    Silence (5 minutes)
    Personal prayers
    Lord's Prayer
    Collect of the week

Day 1:	Psalm 2	Mark 2:15-17
2:	3	Mark 10:23-27
3:	6	Mark 10:46-52
4:	13	Romans 8:1-4
5:	33	Philippians 4:12-13
6:	34	John 11:17-27
7:	43	John 3:16-17

Collect

Most loving Father, whose will it is for us to give thanks for all things, to fear nothing but the loss of you, and to cast all our care on you who care for us: Preserve us from faithless fears and worldly anxieties, that no clouds of this mortal life may hide from us the light of that love which is immortal, and which you have manifested to us in your Son Jesus Christ our Lord; who lives and reigns with you, in the unity of the Holy Spirit, one God, now and for ever. Amen.

Eighth Sunday after the Epiphany (BCP p. 216)

STEP 3
Made a decision to turn our wills and our lives over to the care of God.

Acting on this decision is the hard part. The point of this particular Step is to make the decision to turn our wills and our lives over to the care of God as we understand him. Acting on it comes later.

Christians understand God as revealed in the Holy Trinity. We call God by a variety of names, and God has made himself known to us in a variety of ways: through Jesus Christ, the work of the Holy Spirit, as the love of human beings for others. All those things we attribute to God.

This Step is a very difficult Step because it appears to be like a solid, great oak door that has huge iron hinges and huge iron locks and great bars across it. However, there is a fairly simple key that opens the door. The key is called "willingness." The willingness to do something, the willingness to move forward, is the key. Once this great imposing door is unlocked by the key of willingness, then it almost opens by itself. God moves it aside, so that we can enter into the path that leads to a place that really works.

We are all familiar with the end of the 11th chapter of St. Matthew's Gospel: "Come to me all who labor and are heavy leaden, and I will give you rest. Take my yoke upon you, and learn from me; for I am gentle and lowly in heart, and you will find rest for your souls. For my yoke is easy, and my burden is light." Anybody who comes with any frequency at all to worship God in the Church, can make this Step pretty easily. You may not be there, but you're pretty close. There are few other reasons for coming to church.

As we come to this step, having discussed the first two Steps, questions have been raised: "I'm still at Step 1 or 2"; or you're peeking around the corner at Steps 4, 5, 6, 7 or 8, and "Am I going to get left behind here?" Well, of course you are.

We're all left behind in some place or other, but that's not the point. The introductory work we are doing these 14 weeks is designed to give us a little practice of thinking about different aspects of this search so that in your further development, after this introductory course, you will be able to go back and spend as much time as you and the Lord need to spend on each Step to move from where you are to the next level. What I hope we can do in the process of the course is to convince you to try, and not to be afraid, or at least not so afraid that you're paralyzed. Through disciplined prayer, study time, reading of spiritual writers, and the sharing of your spiritual journey, you will get some practice in both praying and exercising your willingness to come to the Lord.

A Brief Review

Let us review briefly: Step 1 says that we haven't done such a good job in managing our lives, and we certainly haven't done such a good job in managing the lives of those people who are important to us—our loved ones, our spouses our siblings, our children, the people in the church, our best friends. Controlling them hasn't worked. Controlling the economy doesn't work, you just go along with it. You have to buy food, you have to pay the bills, and you don't control it. It mostly controls you. Those inanimate objects take up a lot of your time. Now who's controlling? So, Step 1 is to recognize that life is unmanageable.

When I say life is unmanageable, I don't mean that it is out of control and utter chaos, I mean that much of what is going on around us is just going to happen whether we have any input or not. If you're like I am, the more frantic you get about how things are going to come out, or the more effort you put into it, the worse it turns out. You may get the desired outcome as an end result, but frequently you generate strife and dissension. We haven't done such a good job of managing our lives, but that's not to say that we are awful people—it's just to say, "Hey, I'm not in charge." A mistake I make is believing that I really could control everybody, and that I could live my life without being influenced by my relationships with other people. If we're really in control of ourselves, then we may influence other people but they don't influence us. That's the difference. That doesn't happen. It's coming to realize that we don't exert that power if we try.

Those who have some experience at letting go of the insistence on being in charge discover that they're more influential than they were before, because they are like the eye of a hurricane, they're where the calm, peace and serenity are. Storms may be brewing all around, winds may be 175 knots over there, but right here it's different. From here, you can recognize that you didn't create the world and are not really in charge of it. You have abilities that God gave you, and you may be able to exercise some pretty well, and others not so well. But the world needs to believe that Jesus can do a better job.

I am not asking anybody to go crazy, to say that Jesus directs everything you do. Anybody who claims that is deceived. Many people who say they are being guided by the Son of Light are really not. God doesn't direct personally every little thing you do, whether or not you are going to get a headache, or buy a particular brand of peanut butter. He probably doesn't care what kind of a car you drive.

Step 2 acknowledges, at least intellectually, that Jesus can do a better job. Some of you will be tempted to stop right there. There's this great trap that snaps shut level with our eyes. When our better understanding tells us one thing, the trap prevents it from getting into action at the gut level. Putting a belief into action is not part of Step 2. It's not even part of Step 3.

Time to Decide

Step 3 is when we decide to open the trap door and let a little of God's greatest creation, the brain, leak out into the gut, and begin to turn over our will and our lives to the care of God, the one who nurtures us, creates us, gave us will, gave us our lives, and sent us forth to enjoy the creation and to be stewards of that creation. We have beaten ourselves up, we abuse ourselves, we abuse others, we abuse our will power, and we abuse our lives in all kinds of ways—physically, spiritually, psychologically, from the outside to the inside—and we look at the stories of Jesus and we say, "Jesus was nicer to people than we are. And so, I think maybe I am going to let you start doing a little bit of that for me."

Taking Action

The difficult part is not making the decision, an intellectual exercise, but taking action on the decision and allowing the Lord to actually do something. To think that he can do us good does us no good unless we are willing to give him a chance. I can believe that my wife loves me deeply, but unless I married her, I couldn't really find out for sure. Unless I stay married to her for another 18 years, her love for me may always remain something of a mystery. So we have to take action.

In the Prayer Book that action is called repentance. The baptismal vow is "Whenever we fall into sin we will repent and return to the Lord"— it doesn't say IF we fall into sin, it says WHENEVER we do this. Many times we fail in some way to live a Christian life. In your spiritual journey, whenever you find yourself moving away in another direction, you have vowed to turn back around, face the Lord and return.

This 3rd Step occurs over and over again. It may occur in different parts of my life each day. It may occur in my relationship with my wife one day, my relationship with the children one day, my relationship with you one day, my relationship with myself the other four days. Nobody gets it 100% right the first time; it takes some time.

How Do You Do This?

Does anybody have an idea, a clue, on how you turn your will and your life over to God? How do you do it?

Surrender. That is kind of a military term, isn't it? It either comes when you have been overpowered by the enemy, or you are surrounded without adequate defenses. Surrender is accepting a power greater than yourself taking control. Surrender can also be a positive thing. For instance, lovers surrender to one another in sexual intercourse.

Quit trying to manage everything and let God do his thing for awhile. In doing so, we discover that God is not the enemy, although I'm afraid that we hear that God is sometimes the enemy. One way it is said is that you're all going to hell because you have sinned, and God is glad about that. But if you turn your life over to Jesus you can be spared. Another way you hear it is when some child dies, and people say it is the will of God. We hear that a lot.

There is a lot of goofiness about God, so one of the things we try to do as we grow spiritually is to set aside all of our preconceived and childhood images and to reformulate our beliefs based upon the experience of someone who has peace and serenity in their life. That's part of the purpose of spiritual friendship.

Remember, God created human beings because He delighted in us. God is the one who always tries to reform the community even when everybody has forsaken him and run off. He finds those who have not, collects them up and rebuilds the community. Finally He comes to us in the person of Jesus Christ and brings that message again.

We, in our sinfulness and in our self-will turn around and slam the door shut again. Each time we have to come back and put that key of willingness back in the door, crank it open, and let the Lord back through once again. We frustrate ourselves. We say, "I can't believe I did that; I promised myself I wouldn't do it again, but I did. So now I have to start all over again because obviously I took control and obviously I screwed it up. God didn't make me take control again. God wants to be in control of my life. I believe that in my mind; but I want to be in control of my life, too. So I goofed up and now I have to start all over, go back to Step 1, recognize my own powerlessness, claim again the belief that Jesus can do a better job than I can, make a decision once more to give him another shot at it, even though he goofed up by letting me take control."

Participate in Salvation

Christianity is participatory salvation in which we can do nothing without God, but God will do nothing without us. We cannot earn our own salvation apart from God, but God will not save us unless we participate. First, you can turn yourself over to the care of God in those few minutes you've set aside for your prayer discipline. You can say, "God, I'm going to try this, and I've got fifteen minutes and You can have them. That is the time I'm going to let You do whatever You want to do. I'll allow You to work in my life. I promise I won't run away until the time's up; but when the time's up, I'm out of here." Next, when you're reading your book, say, "Lord, what would You have me hear from this book?" Then maybe you could turn over a relationship that has gone sour and in which you have no hope for reconciliation, say, "Lord, this is eating me up after all these years. Help me to let go of the grudge and to let Your will be done in the relationship." Perhaps you can turn over your ambitions and hopes to the Lord, and start praying that the Lord's will be done. Say, "Your will be done, O Lord. Let my only ambition be to know You. Let Your will prevail in my business life, in my family life, in my public life."

Then, turn over one of your favorite sins, the ones you like. Hebrews calls them the sins that "cling so closely." After that, perhaps you can turn over your concerned intercessions for others, particularly your friends, your family, your enemies, those who wish you harm, a social concern, the state of public schools, the feeding of hungry people, the housing of homeless people, clothing naked people, the deplorable condition of our jails and what they do to people who are already on the wrong track.

Progress, Not Perfection

Begin to pray and turn over your cares and concerns about others. Little by little, you turn a bit more over. It is like the juggler who spins plates on a stick. About the time you have one going well, another one starts wobbling really badly and you have to rush over and get it going again or it will fall off. Turning your will and your life over to the Lord is like that: you really have to pay close attention until it becomes natural and you get good at it. The juggler with the plates on the sticks didn't do twelve the first time. He got one, and then he started to add more. Spiritual growth and growing closer to our Lord takes some practice. The more we practice, the Lord will give more benefits to us and cause us to grow, but it is the Lord who gives the increase.

There are some signs that things are not going well again. We can look for them, like the spinning plates that are starting to get wobbly. Our sign is called "self will run riot." Anger—when you feel rage starting in your abdomen and working its way up through your diaphragm, into your esophagus and up around your lungs—tells you something is wrong in your life. Nobody made you angry. If you say they did, you have surrendered to the wrong power. You choose your response to others. You don't have to submit to a power that is aggravating.

That is not to say that somebody did not do something wrong; but the anger within you is between you and the Lord. Forgiveness does not require the participation of the offender. Forgiveness requires only the participation of the offended person. Reconciliation requires everybody; the forgiveness is something I must do for myself. It is more a gift to myself than it is to anyone else. If I hold a grudge, if I refuse to forgive, then I am the one who suffers both spiritual and physical illness. If I forgive somebody, Jesus says it's like healing, cauterizing and heaping coals of fire on their heads.

Anger, fear, and grudge-bearing are signs of self-will running riot. Arrogance, intolerance, destructiveness of one kind or another, are also signs that we haven't quite finished the job of acting on the decision to turn THAT part of our lives over to the care of God. It's really hard to turn things over that we're really proud of, that we have worked hard for, and accomplish better than anybody else (A's in college, 1600 on the SAT, or whatever it is).

Decide and Act

The decision is just the beginning, the starting place for action. Choosing to leave the building and drive in my car does not get the engine running. I have to leave this room, go out the front door, down to the sidewalk to my car, unlock the door, stick the key in the ignition, turn the ignition and then the engine will run. Only then can I place the car in gear and drive. So making the decision is just the beginning.

There are some growth elements necessary for action. One is disciplined prayer and study. Remember the word "discipline" is the same word as "disciples." It has to do with being a disciple of Christ. Having and being in the company of a spiritual friend also helps us to grow. A spiritual friend is not someone who just says, "Yes, you're a great Christian; you're doing your best." A spiritual friend is somebody who also says, "Wait a minute! What are you talking about? Get real here." He or she reminds you when you start talking about your relationship with your husband or your children or someone else in your life, to remember your relationship with your Lord. When you talk about your laundry and your car, the spiritual friend says, "How is your relationship with your Lord? What is going on between you and your Lord?" The friend helps you to refocus on your spiritual growth.

Talking about the Lord is very difficult for many people. A spiritual friend will help you to learn to talk comfortably, at least in the friend's presence, about your relationship with the Lord. Perhaps you'll never get comfortable doing it any other place, and you don't need to be at the pulpit or on a street corner. If you can talk about the Lord in the presence of your friend, then you're also talking about him in your own presence, and hearing those words come out of your own mouth helps you to grow.

The rest of the Steps continue the work of spiritual growth. Make that decision to turn your wills and your lives over to the care of God as you understand him. Start as big as you can, or as small as you need to. If you don't think God can be trusted, don't give Him but a little bit. Jesus himself said the one who is trustworthy with a little will be given a lot, and if you are untrustworthy with a little you won't be given anything, but that little that will be taken away from you. If it is only a little that you can trust God with, that's all right. If He does all right with it, then give Him a little bit more.

Spiritual Autobiography

This is your homework for this week. In some way, shape, or form, write a spiritual biography. This is not a 4th Step, a fearless and thorough moral inventory. This is a spiritual biography that says this is how the Lord and I have gotten along over the years. You can do it in poetry or in prose, or on a graph.

This is my graph as an example. The horizontal is the time line, and a vertical is positive and negative. I'll share my own spiritual journey as a model. Next week I'll ask you to share yours with your partner. You don't have to tell all, you just say "This is who I am and this is where I have been with Jesus."

First of all, I was born in the church. I have my baptismal certificate hanging on the wall by my desk to remind me when I was a small child, the preacher came over and put water on my head. I was ALWAYS in the church. We went to church and Sunday School, and came back Sunday night to more church, and Wednesday night for prayer meeting. I sang in the choir when I was six years old; I soloed when I was seven. I can still remember being in front of all those people. So as far as I know there has never been a time when I didn't know the Lord.

I go along pretty positive. As I entered my teens things between me and the Lord were pretty good. When I was about 15 I came to believe that I was called for ordained ministry. I went in to talk to the pastor about it, and he was really thrilled about it, so thrilled he told everybody in the church. Things between me and the Lord took a bad turn at that point. Fortunately, my family moved from Garden City, Georgia, to Silver Spring, Maryland. I figured that would provide an escape, because being called to ordained ministry was scary because it was out there on the edge of human-divine relations.

During college, a sense of call came back, and I found another haven in the Episcopal Church. During my junior year, I felt estranged from God. When the "call" returned again, I joined the Air Force to fly combat aircraft.

While in California, my girlfriend asked when I was going to make up my mind about seminary. Since we had not discussed that before, it really startled me. I stopped seeing her and was shortly reassigned.

During my second tour in Vietnam in 1972, I was once again feeling close to the Lord, and a sense of call returned once more. Before I could act on it, I was shot down and captured, serving over three months as a prisoner of war.

When I was repatriated, I attended seminary, a difficult three years of "roller coaster ride" spiritual growth. After ordination, I was assigned to Andrews Air Force Base as a chaplain (1976), and while disenchanted with the chaplaincy, continued to be close to God and grow spiritually. After I left the Air Force, parish life has been filled with ups and downs, but I have been blessed with a peace about the calling, except for a very traumatic year when I was 39.

Briefly, then, that is a sample spiritual biography. Write your own spiritual biography during the next week and be prepared to share with your spiritual friend during the next session.

SPIRITUAL FRIENDSHIP
STEP 3: Made a decision to turn our will and our lives over to the care of God.

Discussion Topics

Share experience of prayer time during past week.

How have you been aware of Jesus' presence in your life this past week?

How have you succeeded (or failed) in deciding to turn your will and your life over to his care?

Share your spiritual biography with your Friend.

SAMPLE PERSONAL RELIGIOUS JOURNEY.

On the chart below I have drawn a solid graph line indicating the various "natural" circumstances of my life. The dashed graph line indicates my religious journey (times when I felt particularly close to or far from God, had a religious awakening, experience, or vision etc.).

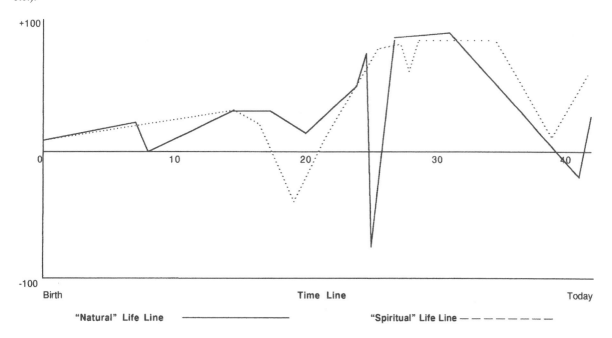

PERSONAL RELIGIOUS JOURNEY.

On the chart below, draw a solid graph line indicating the various "natural" circumstances of your life (birth, moves, schools, loves, deaths, jobs etc.). Draw a dashed graph line indicating your religious journey (times when you felt particularly close to or far from God, had a religious awakening, experience, or vision etc.). Place on the lines special events, places, etc., that help to grow in your Christian faith. What is the relationship between the two life lines? Share your journey with your Spiritual Friend and/or Spiritual Director.

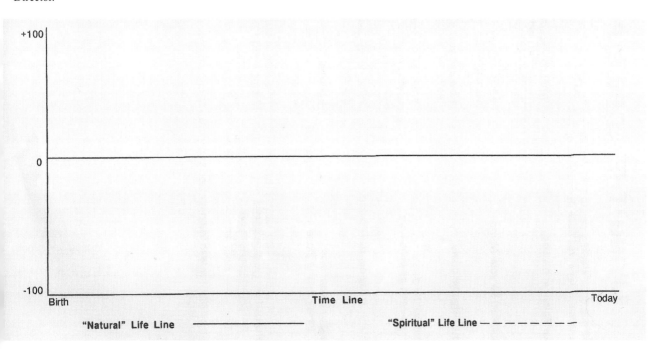

31

LIVING THE LORD'S PRAYER

Here is an interesting way to pray the Lord's Prayer in relation to our lives. These questions might well have been asked by Jesus.

Our Father in heaven, — What do you want to make possible in my life that neither I nor any other human being can make possible?

hallowed be your Name, — What ordinary things in my life do you want to hallow (make holy)?

your kingdom come, — How can your kingdom come through me?

your will be done, — What are my Gethsemanes, about

on earth as in heaven. — which I need to say your will be done?

Give us today our daily bread. — What nourishment or help do I need this day?

Forgive us our sins — For what do I need to be forgiven,
as we forgive those who sin against us. — and for what do I need to forgive others?

Save us from the time of trial, — From what do I need to be protected?
and deliver us from evil.

To be a disciple is to listen for God's response to one's questions and to act accordingly.

¬ John Westerhoff
Used by permission

PRAYER TIME — STEP 3
Theme: Surrender to God.

Step 3: Made a decision to turn our will and our lives over to the care of God.

Format
Preparation (breath prayer, relaxation exercise, etc.)
Read Psalm
Silence (5 minutes)
Read Scripture selection
Silence (5 minutes)
Personal prayers
Lord's Prayer.
Collect of the week

Day 1:	Psalm 23	Romans 12: 1-3
2:	12	Romans 6:12-14
3:	18: 1-20	Colossians 3:12-17
4:	89: 1-18	Matthew 11: 28-30
5:	91	Matthew 7:7-11
6:	95	John 20:26-29
7:	113	Matthew 10: 37-39

Collect
Grant us, O Lord, to trust in you with all our hearts; for, as you always resist the proud who confide in their own strength, so you never forsake those who make their boast of your mercy; through Jesus Christ, your Son our Lord, who lives and reigns with you and the Holy Spirit, one God, now and for ever. Amen.

Proper 18 (BCP p.233)

STEP 4:
Made a searching and fearless moral inventory of ourselves.

In this introduction to spiritual life, everybody's least favorite step is called a "searching and fearless moral inventory," or in more Christian terms, an "examination of conscience." It's a truism, I think, that if you commit a sin once, you think of yourself as a sinner in that regard for the rest of your life. But if you practice a virtue every day of your life, you never think of yourself as particularly virtuous. Isn't that the case? That's how crazy people are.

My experience has been that people are just crazy enough to believe that they are the world's greatest sinners. Or that they have done something original in sinning, and since its original it's not covered by the Scriptures, and so it is somehow outside the realm of forgiveness.

As discussed in the prior Steps, God is not our enemy, holding us at gunpoint to surrender to Him out of defeat. God comes to us as a lover and calls us to risk surrender to Him as the beloved, as a husband and wife surrender to one another in intimacy. There is no need for fear. Moral inventories can be made fearlessly, because we're not doing this in order to be punished. We're doing this in order to find salvation, to find relief from the guilt that we may have been carrying around for all of our lives. Twenty-four hours of guilt is probably enough to cause one to cry for relief.

Sin is Not a Four Letter Word

Sin, and the Greek word for it, means "missing the mark," as in archery. If you don't get a bulls-eye when you're practicing archery, it doesn't mean that you are a miserable failure, it means you didn't get a bulls-eye that time. So you try again. You practice and practice and practice until you get a bulls-eye more regularly. Nobody does it every time, though. Some of the best batters in baseball bat around 300. That is phenomenally good. One out of three times at bat, they actually hit the ball and get on base. Nobody bats a perfect 1000. That's what Paul means when he says, "We have all sinned and fallen short of the glory of God."

What is the issue? One of our baptismal vows says, "Whenever you fall into sin, will you repent and return to the Lord;" it does not say "*If* you ever fall into sin" it says *when* you do it—and you will—will you recognize it; and when you come to recognize it will you repent—which means turn around—and come back to the Lord? So part of what we are after here is to find out where we have turned the wrong direction so that we can turn back around. If we go around in total denial like the Pharisee in the story of the Pharisee and the publican, and say, "Thank God I'm not a sinner like that publican over there," then we are in denial and not recognizing the truth. As Paul says later, "If we say that we have no sin, the truth is not in us." First we have to recognize that we all have fallen short, there are places where we have turned the wrong way. Then we must turn back to our intended course.

If you get on the interstate in Memphis, Tennessee, to take somebody to the Little Rock, Arkansas airport, and turn east, and as you pass Lakeland you keep going, it does no good to say, "Gee, I'm sorry. I know I am on the right interstate, but we don't seem to be getting any closer to Little Rock." If you keep traveling, it doesn't do any good. Instead, you have to get off the interstate somewhere down the line, turn around and go back to the west, because the Little Rock airport is not east of Memphis. Little Rock will not move to the east just because were going that way. Our trip is not going to turn out all right if we get to Nashville, because that is not our destination. Turning around is the sign of repentance. Sin might be described as a virtue turned inside out. The good intent was to take your friend to the Little Rock airport. That virtue got turned around backwards and you wound up in Nashville or Knoxville or Bristol or Washington, D.C. if you carry the sin far enough.

Step 4, a vigorous and painstaking effort to discover where we have turned things awry, helps us discover where our assets have been turned into liabilities. We also rediscover some assets that were always there that have not been used in a while. An inventory is not just pitching everything out of the window for the garbage man to carry away; it is looking over everything that's present in our moral lives, and determining what is useful and what is not useful, what is helpful and what is harmful. Take the useless stuff and the harmful stuff and pitch those out for the garbage man to carry away, and keep the good stuff, the useful stuff, the things we want to carry with us some more.

Some Helpful Questions

Some questions might help us identify examples of virtues turned into liabilities. How have we warped our virtues, how have our virtues become skewed and turned inside out? How have we hurt others, caused damage to other people? For instance, it is a God-given gift to human beings that we have a need to both love and be loved by others. That's a gift. It is a virtue to love another person, it is a great blessing to be loved by another. But that instinct and virtue taken to the extreme of exclusiveness and distortion turns into sexual promiscuity, infidelity and possessiveness. Lots of people get into that cycle. The harvest of distorted love in our time is an increase of penicillin resistant strains of the venereal diseases, the spread of AIDS and other diseases that are destroying bodies. We also know that the virtue of love taken in this distorted way destroys relationships, builds huge amounts of guilt on top of people's shoulders, causes loss of jobs, marriages, and friends.

Another basic human trait is the need for security, to have some sense that I am secure in my person, that I have a secure place to bed down at night, a place to be out of the weather. Security run amok turns someone into a workaholic or a miserly, stingy person who grasps everything that he or she can, and gives nothing away or shares nothing with anyone else. It turns others into the bully who is so insecure in and of their own person that they have to shove other people around and scare other people, make them afraid. The bully becomes less vulnerable to attack, because people become unwilling, or afraid to come near.

Another way to become secure is, like Howard Hughes, to become a hermit and completely separate yourself from other people. If you don't open yourself up to being hurt by engaging in any relationship whatsoever, then you're not going to get hurt. However, you're not going to get loved a lot either. Howard Hughes was very wealthy, but what good did it do him? He had lots of money, lots of businesses, lots of wealth, but nothing else. He had gained the world and lost his soul.

I believe that God would have us be successful. I think it is the Hebrew and Christian understanding that fidelity leads to success in life; but success can be turned into sin when people strive for success by cheating, destroying others, lying, and stealing. It starts out as a virtue, but turns into a sin.

Guilt—Some Good, Some Bad

The result of disfigured instincts and virtues is that relationships become stressed and broken. We blame other people for the bad things that happen to us. "It was somebody else's fault that my stock went under. It was somebody else's fault that I was in that wreck." Refusal to accept personal responsibility further breaks down our relationships. We either blame others and spray the world like a skunk, or turn our loathing in on ourselves and feel guilty, self loathing, and inappropriate and misplaced guilt.

There are things for which we *should* feel guilty, but more often than not, we tend to be more plagued by misplaced and neurotic guilt. It's like the people that you read about every once in awhile that confess to crimes they didn't commit so they can be punished. They really feel guilty about somebody being murdered over in the next neighborhood, or an earthquake killing people in California, or a volcano in Colombia. They feel guilty, as though they had somehow caused it because they didn't pray right or something.

There is, however, real sin in the world, too. We have participated in some of it; we have probably participated a lot less than some of us think we have. We also have participated in sin that we deny. The purpose of Step 4, the moral inventory, the examination of conscience, is to get in and start sorting our lives out. It is a lonely thing that we do because we are not yet at Step 5. Step 4 is something you do with yourself. An inventory asked the question, "What's in the closet? What's in the attic? What's good as well as what's bad in there"? An inventory asks, "What in all of this stuff really belongs to me, and what belongs to someone else?" For instance, children who are sexually abused by their parents carry guilt around about it. That guilt doesn't belong to the abused person; that guilt belongs to the abuser. And so we have to begin to say, "You know, an innocent has no responsibility for that. The adult has a great deal of responsibility, but the holy innocent doesn't, the innocent is the victim here."

There is a sense in which, if you have ever had a house robbery, you feel violated and guilty. You start saying things like, "I should have locked the door, or had bars, or had an alarm." When my family was robbed, our experience was that the fear didn't go away right away, it stayed around and some of the self-blaming lingered. "You should have had a deadbolt installed earlier, you shouldn't have had the drapes open, or shouldn't have been away from the house." That doesn't belong to us. The danger is a break-down in basic trust. I'm not sure it's ever a simple thing to trust other human beings to be honest. It may be stupid, but I don't think it's sinful.

"Spring Cleaning"

So the inventory is designed as preparation to take the garbage to the dump. In that garbage there are all kinds of things, vengeful resentments directed toward others, self-pity ("We're such maligned individuals and don't have the benefit of others"), unwarranted pride ("We're such terrific individuals"), and all that sort of garbage in life.

It is a whole lot easier to see the garbage in somebody else's house than it is to see it in your own. My house is comfortably lived in, your house is a mess. Jesus says, how can you dare to presume to remove a speck of dust out of somebody else's eye, when you have this tree lodged in your own. It's a lot easier to take somebody else's inventory. Resist the temptation to do that. Don't take your Spiritual Friend's inventory, take your own.

Seven Deadly Sins

In Christian understanding there are Seven Deadly Sins: pride, envy, sloth, greed, lust, anger and gluttony. Some of you may be familiar with a devotional guide published by the Order of the Holy Cross called the *St. Augustine's Prayer Book*. This little prayer book has a lot of things in it, and among them is an examination of conscience based on the Ten Commandments and the Seven Deadly Sins. I have adapted the list to make it a moral inventory by including questions designed to elicit your virtues as well as your sins. Let me go over that with you in some detail, because this is the guide I'm offering you to help you through the next week.

What's Next?

Next week we will talk about private confession, and a 5th Step, which is "admitted to ourselves, to God and to another human being the exact nature of our wrongs." The 6th and 7th Steps also fit in with a private confession, too. You may find that you can do the inventory in one sitting, although I think that if you have a day or a half a day that you can really devote to going back over your life since your last confession, then go back, because there may be stuff that you'll discover in the back of your closet that really bothers you and that you might have put in the back of your memory for some time. It comes up in concentrated searching and house cleaning so you can get rid of it.

The Inventory

Read the inventory. First of all, there's a prayer that's offered here to be said, as you begin this process. Any time you sit down, if it takes you 10 sittings to accomplish it, that's OK, but just say the prayer first. Notice how the prayer is written, "Holy Spirit, source of all life, source of wisdom, of understanding, of knowledge, come to my assistance; enable me to make a good confession. Enlighten me." "Permit me not to be blinded." And so on.

Then there are rubrics that give some instructions on how to approach this task. "Think of yourself as God's child." The wickedness of following Satan is out there to be done, it's true, but that's not what you're here for. You're not followers of Satan, you're not chasing after Lucifer. You may have discovered that you have taken a step or two in that direction at one time or another, but that's not what's important. Think of yourself as a child of God.

Don't be in a hurry, and don't worry yourself because you can't remember everything. There are some things that you will not be able to bring out of memory. That's okay. But the important thing is to be honest with yourself. If you know there's something hidden behind a curtain, push the curtain aside and get it out. Put it down on paper. It will not hurt you, unless you leave it behind a curtain. It's a bogeyman, it's like the little boy with the anxiety closet in that cartoon strip, Bloom County. If you leave it in the closet, it will stay there to creep out at you at night; and it will continue to be there, nagging at you, until you get it out in the open.

The sunlight, whether you spell it sunlight or sonlight, the judgment of Christ, is like sun entering a dark room, bringing a candle into the house so that it casts light into the corners. If you'll remember as a little child, what you wanted most when you were scared at night was for the light to come on, so that you could see what was making the shadows. Usually, what was making shadows was quite small. Remember the Wizard of Oz was not a great terrible creature, he was a little gnome, who had a light behind him to cast a shadow on the curtain so that everybody would think he was a great terrible creature. Satan is like that; Satan has no power whatsoever, period, except lies and deception.

If there is something telling you that there's a great enormous sin hidden in your life, and that if you ever get it out it'll kill you, that's Satan lying to you. Don't worry about that stuff. Just be honest. One of the reasons in AA why people can't get past or will never do a 4th Step, is because they don't want to do a 5th Step. They get bogged down talking about the 5th Step as a way of avoiding the 4th Step. Let's try to avoid doing that. Take seriously the little statement, "Do not fret about your sins." Circle it in red, underline it in purple or something.

It does say write them down; but I am going to say now, and I'll say it again, secure what you write. Take it in shorthand, lock it in a safe deposit box, put it where nobody else is going to find it, keep it on your person at all times. This is not for anybody else's consumption. This is not the beginning of a book. The reason why you write it down is so you don't have to rely on your memory so much when you get to the 5th Step. You don't have to write it down in graphic detail, trigger words will do. It can be encoded as long as you understand what it means so that you don't accidentally forget something later, which is what we call denial and avoidance. Remember, you are trying to recall these things in order that you may be forgiven, not that you may be condemned. God does not despise a broken and contrite heart.

What's the Point?

The purpose here is to alleviate depression, or prevent it from occurring, to quiet guilt that does not belong to you, and to heal guilt that does. The guide here suggests some possible questions for getting at some of the stuff. You may not qualify for all the questions. Don't worry about it. If you don't understand a question or if it doesn't apply, don't try to force something to apply to it so that you can have a longer list than somebody else. Just answer the questions honestly. Honestly search your closets and under your bed and behind the curtains and in the attic and in the garage and wherever else things are stuffed around in your spiritual life. This is a *complete* inventory.

Pride and Humility. There are a lot of ways in which we show pride. It is connected to that first commandment of having no other gods, but the one God. That's putting yourself there, your spouse there, or your children, or your careers, or your clothes, or your money, or your jewelry, or your apartment, or your home, or your front yard, or whatever it is that gets between you and your Lord, that puts God somewhere other than in first place.

Idolatry and Single-Minded Devotion. We have all kinds of ways of making idols. You can make an idol out of a church. You can make an idol out of your prayer life, like the Pharisee and the publican. The Pharisee's obedience to Torah became more important than his love of God, and his honesty before God.

Profanity and Godliness. Probably the most profane thing we do is claim as God's will our own selfish purposes. Nazi soldiers in World War II had belt buckles that said "God is with us." The Crusades were all in the name of God to liberate Jerusalem from the heathen. There are all kinds of ways of misusing the name of God. I've heard people say that it was the Lord's will that they be greedy and take a $300,000 bonus at Christmas, and a $6 million a year salary. It's the Lord's will, fill in the blank. I have heard that stuff until I'm sick of it, and I think it's profanity. I think it's profanity and blasphemy, for instance, when somebody says it's the Lord's will that some baby died, or some teenager wound up on drugs. I can't find an example in Jesus' ministry were Jesus killed a live person or made sick a healthy person; but I can find all kinds of examples where he raised the dead and healed the sick. Profanity is using the Lord's name in vain ways, that are not God's ways.

Irreverence and Reverence. Keep holy the Sabbath day, or in Christian practice, the Lord's Day. The Sabbath is still Saturday; Christians meet for worship on the Lord's Day, the first day of creation and the day of resurrection. God created rest and gave us a day of rest in order that we not make an idol of work, but have a time when we simply enjoy life. Keeping holy the Sabbath day has to do with both the Sabbath and the Lord's Day. Holy days are kept in order that all of life may become holy. The questions here have to do with not keeping the Lord's Day, but also with being irreverent when you are at worship, or joking about holy things, or being ashamed of your religion, or ashamed of your Lord.

Disobedience and Gratitude. Honor thy father and thy mother. There is a book called *Out of the House of Slavery* by Brian Haggerty, a Jesuit priest who proposes the different translation of this Commandment, more accurate to the time in the Hebrew exodus and to the understanding of Hebrew community. It is not what we as Christians think. In Judaism, on the two tablets, there are five Commandments on the left and five on the right; in Christian renderings of the Ten Commandments there are four on the left and six on the right. The Hebrews put this commandment to honor father and mother on the tablet that has to do with our relationship with God. We put it on the side that has to do with our relationship with other people. Haggerty is saying that a better translation is "show deference to the elderly because they are the

38

repositories of the memory of who you are. They are the storytellers, the tradition bearers. It is tradition that tells us that we are at the beloved children of God, the creation of God. The elders of the community have the responsibility of transmitting the tradition. So it's not just the mother and father, but the elders of the community who are the ones who teach the faith.

Hate and Love. Committing murder takes many forms other than the destruction of another human body. Grudge-bearing and refusing to forgive is perhaps the most insidious in that it will destroy the bearer's body and soul. Gossip and slander murders a person's reputation and character, divides communities, and endangers friendships. Racial and ethnic prejudice denies God as creator, Jesus as redeemer, and the Holy Spirit and the light of all humanity. Blindness to human suffering contributes to the death of body and spirit.

Impurity and Chastity. In Christian marriage, we give ourselves—body, mind, and soul—to one other person. Withholding encouragement, compassion, financial resources, as well as sexual union is a denial of our vows. Giving emotional and physical love to another person while denying our life partner that same love is adultery. Impurity takes more forms than sexual union apart from the marriage bed. Overindulgence in food, sex, alcohol, work, play or any other facet of life is also abusive of the human body (the temple of God).

Theft and Honesty. As with the other commandments, let us not narrowly define stealing. Theft includes much more than taking some physical thing from another. It also includes lying, which robs others of truth and reality. It includes cheating, which denies fairness to others. Spending too much denies you and your family the money to buy the necessities of life. Failure to tithe is stealing from God and preventing Christ's Church from growing and from assisting those in need.

Deceit and Openness. Speaking a lie is the most obvious form of bearing false witness; but withholding the truth, or speaking partial truth is more destructive. Also included under this commandment are insults and putdowns which are lies and distortions of another person's character.

Discontent and Satisfaction. Jealousy of another person's possessions is a denial of the worth of your own and a rejection of your own redemption. If you reject what you have, you are rejecting reality and preventing your own growth. Accepting your lot in life, coupled with trust in God to cause "all things to work together for good" provides you with the building blocks for better future. You cannot start a journey from where you wish you were; you can only start from where you are. Accepting your own starting place does not mean you have to stay there; it means that you are now free to change and grow. Satisfaction does not mean sitting in the trash heap, smiling dumbly; it means searching through that "trash heap" for usable resources and working with God to turn them into assets.

Finally, having made a fearless and thorough inventory, thank God that he has given you much that is good and promised to heal what is broken and to remove what is damaging. You will then be ready to take the next 3 Steps with joyful anticipation.

SPIRITUAL FRIENDSHIP
Step 4: Made a searching and fearless moral inventory of ourselves.

Discussion Topics
 Share experience of prayer time during past week.
 Share experience (not specifics) of making a moral inventory.
 Was it an experience of grace? Guilt?
 How did you feel in your relationship with Jesus during this process?
 Were you closer? Estranged?
 Discuss your spiritual reading.
 How are you feeling about your Friendship relationship?

FROM THE EXHORTATION

Judge yourselves, therefore, lest you be judged by the Lord.

Examine your lives and conduct by the rule of God's commandments, that you may perceive, wherein you have offended in what you have done or left undone, whether in thought, word, or deed. Acknowledge your sins before Almighty God, with full purpose of amendment of life, being ready to make restitution for all injuries and wrongs done by you to others; and also being ready to forgive those who have offended you, in order that you yourselves may be forgiven.

And if, in your preparation, you need help and counsel, then go and open your grief to a discreet and understanding priest, and confess your sins, that you may receive the benefit of absolution, and spiritual counsel and advice; to the removal of scruple and doubt, the assurance of pardon, and the strengthening of your faith.

Book of Common Prayer, p. 316 — 317

A GUIDE FOR SELF EXAMINATION.
(A SEARCHING AND FEARLESS MORAL INVENTORY)
(Adapted from *St. Augustine's prayer book,* copyright Holy Cross publications, 1967)

Before self examination, say this prayer:

O Holy Spirit, Source of all light, Spirit of wisdom, of understanding, and of knowledge, come to my assistance and enable me to make a good inventory. Enlighten me, and help me now to know my sins and my virtues as one day I shall know them fully before your judgment seat. Bring to my mind both the evil and the good which I have done. Reveal the sin I have avoided and the good which I have neglected. Permit me not to be blinded by self-love or by shame. Grant me, moreover, heartfelt sorrow for my sins and shortcomings, knowing how deeply they have wounded a loving heart of my heavenly Father; and help me to make a good confession that all stain of guilt may be washed away in the precious blood of my Savior Jesus Christ. Amen.

Think of yourself as God's child, and of the wickedness of following Satan rather than your loving father.

Do not be in a hurry, do not worry yourself because you cannot remember everything. Be honest with God and with yourself; this is all God asks of you.

Write down briefly what you remember of your sins and your virtues. Don't try to depend on your memory. If there is any question you do not understand, let it alone, and go onto the next one.

Do not fret about your sins. Remember, you are trying to recall them in order that you may be forgiven, not that you may be condemned. "A broken and contrite heart, O God, shalt thou not despise."

Do not be puffed up with pride about your virtues. Remember that they are from God and that you are the steward of those gifts.

I. PRIDE/HUMILITY.

You shall have no other gods, but me.

Have you been more interested in self than in God?

As you may need your chief aim to be always on top?

What have you been vain about; personal appearance, clothes, personality, possessions, your family, ability, success in games or in studies?

Have you scorned other people for their misfortunes, their sins, stupidity, or other weaknesses?

Scorned other people's religion?

Talked too much; called attention to yourself?

Been sorry for yourself, self-pitying?

Refused to admit when you are in the wrong? Refused to apologize?

Been resentful or suspicious of others through over-sensitiveness?

Have you been stubborn and self-willed? In what ways?

How have you sought the Lord's guidance and will for yourself? In your relationships?

How have you placed others before yourself?

How have you sought to be helpful to others for the upbuilding of the Church?

What have you done to overcome estrangement?

II. IDOLATRY/SINGLE-MINDED DEVOTION

You shall not make for yourself any idol.

Have you put another person before God, by not going to church, or by committing some other sin to please that person?

Have you wanted popularity so much that you have not said your prayers, or done some other good things, for fear of being laughed at?

Have you loved money or clothes too much; or even sinned to get them?

Have you gone to mediums, fortune tellers or astrologers?

How do you understand yourself as steward instead of owner of the things and people in your life?

How do you maintain your relationship with the Lord?

III. PROFANITY/GODLINESS.

You shall not invoke with malice, the name of the Lord your God.

Have you misused the holy name of Jesus?

Have you given way to anxiety, instead of turning to God for help?

Have you been worried, afraid, allowed yourself to get into a panic?

Have you allowed yourself to feel it was impossible even for God to help you?

Have you claimed as "God's will" your own selfish purposes?

How have you proclaimed by word and example the good news of God in Christ?

How have you relied on the Lord in times of stress?

How have you set your desires aside in order to do the Christ-like thing?

IV. IRREVERENCE/REVERENCE.

Remember the Sabbath day and keep it holy.

Have you missed the holy Eucharist on Sunday, when you could've gone?

Have you failed to say your prayers? Or to say them earnestly?

Have you always kept Sunday as the Lord's Day?

Have you done some unnecessary work on Sunday?

Have you always tried hard to worship God when in church? Or have you sometimes been irreverent? Or joked about holy things?

Have you ever been ashamed of your religion? Of Jesus?

How do you "continue in Apostles' teaching and fellowship, the breaking of bread, and in the prayers"?

How do you maintain your relationship with the Lord through your personal prayers and reading?

How do you use your God-given talents and abilities for the upbuilding of the church?

V. DISOBEDIENCE/GRATITUDE

Honor your father and your mother.

Have you been grateful enough for the good that your elders have done for you?

Have you been open and willing to learn of their faith?

Have your actions ever caused them anxiety or shame?

Have you ever shown disregard for the traditions of the church? For the laws of the land?

What sins have you committed with regard to your spouse, children, or other members of your family?

43

Have you given as much care and attention as possible to the religious life of your family?

Have you seen that your children had adequate and continuous religious instruction?

Have you been just and generous to people in your employment, or under your authority in business? In what ways have you failed?

Have you tried to dominate the lives of others unduly? How?

How have you sought to learn from others?

How have you sought Christ in all persons?

How have you taught others about Christ?

How have you shared your faith with others?

How have you respected the dignity of every human being?

VI. HATE/LOVE.

You shall not commit murder.

Have you killed anyone, either in outward deed, or in your heart?

Have you wished that someone was dead?

Have you been angry unjustly? Struck people? Or hurt them by ridicule or contempt?

Have you ever cursed people?

Have you ever gossiped about people?

Is there anyone whom you now hold a grudge against? Or are unwilling to forgive?

Have you refused to help people who were in real need of help? Ignored the sick or the poor?

Not tried to be friendly with people, especially with people who are not very popular?

Have you been afraid to stand up for a person when others were mistreating him?

Have you ever taught (or tempted) another person to sin?

What do you do to overcome your prejudices?

How have you sought to be reconciled with others?

How have you forgiven others? Sought the forgiveness of others?

How have you helped others who are less (more) fortunate than you? Different from you?

How have you tried to confront gossip or prejudice by others?

VII. IMPURITY/CHASTITY

You shall not commit adultery.

Have you been impure in thought, word, or deed? Alone? With another person? Man or woman?

Have you looked at pictures or read books out of sexual lust?

Have you been immodest in actions, or in dress?

Have you been lazy in prayers, work, or study? Neglected business, family, or social duties?

Have you eaten, drank, or smoked more than was good for you?

Have you neglected the days of fasting or abstinence? (see BCP p. 17)

Have you broken rules or resolutions which you have made for yourself?

Allowed yourself to be over-engrossed in light reading, the movies, television, or other pastimes, to the exclusion of worthwhile things?

Have you been cowardly in sickness or pain?

Have you been unmindful of the suffering of the world?

44

How do you maintain the fitness of your body?

Are you faithful to your spouse? Sexually? Emotionally? Psychologically?

How have you been diligent in the performance of your duties?

How do you contribute to the overall health of the community in which you live?

VIII. THEFT/HONESTY

You shall not steal.

Have you ever stolen anything? What things? Have you shared in stolen goods?

Have you cheated in business, games, or lessons?

Have you been over-extravagant; gambled or bet too much?

Tried hard to pay all your debts? Contracted debts unnecessarily?

Have you remembered that God has given you all you have? Have you thanked Him enough?

Have you given as much as you ought to the Church or to charities?

Have you been stingy?

Have you wasted time?

Are you honest when no one is looking?

IX. DECEIT/OPENNESS

You shall not be a false witness.

Have you told lies? What were they?

Have you exaggerated too much? Been deceitful, unfair, a hypocrite?

Allowed others to receive blame for your faults?

Been harsh toward others, or in speaking of others, for sins which you also have committed?

Have you come to the defense of someone who has been unjustly accused?

Have you spoken the truth when it was unpopular or inconvenient?

Have you forgiven others for their failures and sins?

X. DISCONTENT/SATISFACTION

You shall not covet anything that belongs to your neighbor.

Have you been jealous of others because they had more things, or more money; or because
     they were better looking or more successful; or because someone loves them more than you?

Been grieved at the prosperity or attainments of others?

Been dejected because of the position, talents, or fortune of others?

Have you been glad when they failed, or were in trouble? Glad when you heard people speak
     ill of them?

Have you allowed yourself to be sad and discouraged at times; and not always fought to be
     brave and joyful?

Have you tried to accept loss or sorrow or hard things, trusting that God would help you
     through it?

Have you thought that God does not love you?

Have you ever given up trying to be good?

Have you rejoiced over the good fortune of others?

Have you offered congratulations to someone who has succeeded at something?
Have you offered empathy and help to someone who has failed?
Are you grateful for your talents, abilities, and successes?

Prayer after Self-Examination

O my God, how great are my sins! Would that I had never offended You. If by carelessness or ignorance I have forgotten anything in my self-examination, show it to me now that I may make a good confession. I thank You for the blessing of family and friends, and for the loving care which surrounds me on every side. I thank You for setting me at tasks which demand my best efforts and for leading me to accomplishments which satisfy and delight me. I thank You also for those disappointments and failures that lead me to acknowledge my dependence on You alone. Grant me the gift of Your Spirit, that I may find forgiveness for my sins, strength in my weakness, and praise for You in my heart, through Jesus Christ our Lord. Amen.

PRAYER TIME - STEP 4

Theme: Examination of Conscience

Step 4:   Made a searching and fearless moral inventory of ourselves.

Format
    Preparation (breath prayer, relaxation exercise, etc)
    Read Psalm
    Silence (5 minutes)
    Read Scripture selection
    Silence (5 minutes)
    Personal prayers
    Lord's Prayer
    Collect of the week

Day 1:	Psalm 139	Daniel 9:4-7
2:	24	I John 2:1-5
3:	32	Matthew 7:1-5
4:	36	Luke 18:9-14
5:	90	I John 1:5-10
6:	119:169-176	Luke 14:28-33
7:	143	Luke 6:37-38

Collect
    Almighty and most merciful God, kindle within us the fire of love, that by its cleansing flame we may be purged of all our sins and made worthy to worship You in spirit and in truth; through Jesus Christ our Lord. Amen.

Collect for *Lent and other times of penitence*, (BCP, p. 111)

THIS WEEK: Conduct a moral inventory. Write it down. Keep it secure.

STEP 5:
Admitted to God, to ourselves, and to another human being
the exact nature of our wrongs.

Spiritual growth is reversing the sin of First Man/First Woman. In the Genesis story, the first sin was the eating of the fruit of the tree of the knowledge of good and evil. The seduction by Satan was, "It'll be good for you. It's not evil, it's good. It will make you like God." The tragedy was that they somehow failed to notice, or had forgotten, that on the sixth day of creation, when God created First Man/First Woman, God created them in his own image. We were already in the image and likeness of God. Therefore, grasping for Godhood was the sin of First Man/First Woman; and spiritual growth is to reverse that sin, to deflate the ego and, instead of always trying to be God, to let God be God, and take on the role of God's beloved creation, God's partners, but nevertheless, God's servants and stewards.

Hard Work

Here in the middle of the 12 Steps, we get into the really hard, difficult pieces that go to work on this sinful inclination to do the evil thing. It is hard work. It creates all kinds of anxiety because one of the lies that Satan has told us is that if anybody ever finds out about our sin, they'll excommunicate us, they'll cut off the relationship with us, they won't love us. If they ever know what we're really like on the inside, then we would have no friends at all. All this is a lie. The reason that it is so difficult for everybody the first time we really decide to go in and do some house-cleaning, some sweeping up, some straightening up, in our own interior is because we have all these lies that the unfriendly spirit has told us. We have to overcome them to get back into the task. It gets real easy after you've done it a few times.

There is always a danger when growth starts in earnest. Satan will sneak in there any old way he can. One of those ways is to get you familiar and comfortable with your spiritual growth and lead you to make a generic confession: "I was prideful." But Step 5 is substance and difficult. However, just as Step 4 was as much an experience of grace as it was an experience of being confronted with guilt and with some unhappy things in your life, so Step 5 is very similar. It is very scary because you move from being on the paper to saying it out loud where you can hear it, where another human being can hear it, and obviously where God can hear it. It is scary, I won't deny that, but it will not kill you. In fact, making a good clean confession results in a sense of great relief.

If you ever go river-rafting you get all your clothes soaking wet and you have to stay in them for several hours. You get used to the weight of those wet clothes and when you take them off you feel a lot lighter. If you're toting a heavy load, you get used to it and you don't even notice it any more. When you take it off, put down the burden, you feel a lot lighter. Well, that's what happens with Step 5. It is a major bridge in life to true kinship with God as well as with other people.

Even though we don't confess all of our sins and wickedness to everybody we know, having made a good, clean, honest confession in a lot of those relationships that have become strained are bridged over. It gets rid of the dirty little secrets. The thing about dirty little secrets is that sometimes we feel like we're transparent and people can see them, and we're really afraid of them. So we begin to build a wall around ourselves so that people can see less of us. We're afraid they're going to find out about one little thing that happened to us, or that we did, or failed to do, so we start building walls around us for protection. When we do that, we put greater distance between us and other human beings, and we find that we cannot have relationships that are really intimate anymore, because the wall is there.

BENEFITS
Taking Down Walls
Once we get rid of the dirty little secret by giving it back to God in confession and burning the paper, then the absence of the dirty little secret begins to cause the wall to just melt away. We feel more self-confident, we feel better about ourselves, we experience the grace of God more deeply, and so the fear we have of relationships with other people begins to melt away. Even though we're not going to tell anyone else what the secret was, because it's not a secret anymore, it no longer matters.

A Change in Constitution
Once we've been forgiven and the guilt has been taken away sacramentally, it is no longer a part of who we are. That piece of inventory has been tossed away, so it is no longer ours. It clearly leads to real forgiveness and the next step beyond that, to reconciliation. Forgiveness and reconciliation result from the 5th Step.

Humility
Another benefit and virtue that counteracts pride is a real sense of humility. Humility comes from at least two directions. One is recognizing and having said in another person's presence what our sins are, so we can clearly see our true character. The other direction is that we discover that we're not original. Some of us may think that we are the world's worst at whatever our favorite sin is, the one that clings so closely. Then we discover that the priest is not particularly shocked. He or she has probably heard it before. We did not think it up or originate it; others have done it before. We also have not been condemned, even though for years we may have thought one thing we had done when we were 18 years old was the one sin that God would never forgive in anybody.

Humility comes because we discover that we are not the world's chief sinners. Paul claimed that for himself, but he was being very prideful when he did it. He also sounds prideful when he says, "Thank God, I never baptized one of you—except Crispus and Gaius. So no one can say you were baptized in my name. Yes, I did baptize the household of Stephanas: I cannot think of anyone else." (I Corinthians 1:14-16) The trouble with papyrus was that it was so expensive that you couldn't throw it away or go back and erase something already written.

New Understanding
Honest self-evaluation leads to a certain reality about ourselves that says, "Yes, I am a sinful person but I am also a virtuous person and the two poles are fighting within me." Paul speaks of this trouble when he says, "The good that I would do, I do not do, and the evil I hate is the very thing I wind up doing." So, yes, it is true we are sinners, but it is also true that we are the beloved children of God. The sense of being loved is reinforced in us in the process of sacramental confession. If we have known it before, or if we know it in our heads, but have not experienced it in our hearts or in our guts, then the act of Reconciliation helps to diffuse the love of God throughout our being.

Tranquility
The sacramental act of reconciliation leads us through honest evaluation to another miracle of life, a certain level of tranquility or serenity in the presence of God and a consciousness of God in our daily lives. That's where we're going in this Quest.

Baptismal Expectations

Let's look at the Prayer Book and see what it says. Look first at page 304 in the covenant of the baptismal liturgy. An example of what the Church expects about your ability to withstand sin is found in the last vow on that page: "Will you persevere in resisting evil, and whenever you fall into sin repent and return to the Lord?" It doesn't say "IF you fall into sin after baptism, will you repent and return to the Lord." It says "WHEN" you do it. So the Church, the Body of Christ, does not expect you to be sinless from the time of baptism. That was Constantine's concern, so he waited until he was nearly dead before he was baptized. But we are a little more realistic than that. We would hate for somebody not to be baptized just because they're afraid they're going to sin again, because we can guarantee that the sin will occur. The other important clause of this vow is, instead of doing like many people do when they discover their post-baptismal sin, "Will you repent (turn around) and return to the Lord?" Do not say, "Oh gosh, I've done this awful thing, so I can't be part of the church anymore. They won't like me, or it's just scandal." In our Baptisms, then, we recognize that we will sin again; but we promise God and the Church that we will continue to seek forgiveness and reconciliation.

The Need for Examination and Reconciliation

Turn now to page 316, the Exhortation. It starts by alluding to the words of Paul in the I Corinthians 11:27-32, He who eats and drinks, eats and drinks judgment on himself if he does not discern the Body. That is why many of you are feeble and sick, and a number have died." The important point for us is, "Examine your lives and conduct by the rule of God's commandments, (that's what we did in the 4th Step) that you may perceive wherein you have offended in what you have done or left undone... acknowledge your sins before Almighty God with full purpose of amendment in life, (here we are getting into the 5th Step). Being ready to make restitution for all injuries or wrongs done by you to others; (that's getting on to the 8th and 9th Steps). And also being ready to forgive those who have offended you in order that you yourselves may be forgiven." We read in the next paragraph, "If, in your preparation, you need help and counsel, then go and open your grief to a discreet and understanding priest and confess your sins that you may (here are the benefits) receive the benefit of absolution, spiritual counsel and advice; to the removal of scruple and doubt, the assurance of pardon, and the strengthening of your faith."

Why Confession?

Those are the reasons we go to private confession, we do not go to be embarrassed or condemned. We do not go to be beaten with a cat-of-nine-tails and given great and notorious penance. We go in order to have scruple (over-attention to moral standards) reduced, to remove doubt of our own salvation, to be assured of pardon for the wrongs we have done, and to have our faith strengthened. So that is what the Exhortation tells us that private confession is all about.

A Rule of Thumb

The Anglican rule of thumb that derives from the Exhortation is that "confession is open to all, is necessary for some, but is required for none." It is open to all, any time you desire it. It is necessary for some in order to have concerns alleviated any time we are unable to find relief alone. Then we need to seek out a priest. When we attempt to alleviate our guilt by burying our sins in the back of the closet, they don't go away. They sneak out from time to time and grab us and raise our anxiety level and guilt a lot higher.

What Happens?

For those of you have never participated in the Reconciliation of a Penitent, let us discuss exactly what happens. Turn to page 446, a page entitled "Concerning the Rite." Always read these pages in the Prayer Book because they tell you what is intended and what is going to happen. "The ministry of reconciliation, which has been committed by Christ to his Church, is exercised through the care each Christian has for others, through the common prayer of Christians assembled for public worship, and through the priesthood of the Church and its ministers declaring absolution. The Reconciliation of a Penitent is available for all who desire it. It is not restricted to times of sickness. Confessions may be heard anytime and anywhere. Two equivalent forms of service are provided here to meet the needs of penitents." The expression of things is a little different in each one, so you will want to read through them both so you can choose which one really says what you want to say. "The absolution in these services may be pronounced only by a bishop or priest. Another Christian may be asked to hear a confession, but it must be made clear to the penitent that absolution will not be pronounced; instead, a declaration of forgiveness is provided."

On the bottom of page 448 there is a Declaration of Forgiveness to be used by a Deacon or Lay Person, which says "Our Lord Jesus Christ, who offered himself to be sacrificed for us to the Father, forgives your sins by the grace of the Holy Spirit." This is an acceptable and authorized form, but it is not of the same impact as having the priest say to you, "by His Authority committed to me, I absolve you from all your sins." For those in 12 Step programs, 5th Step sponsors may find this to be a helpful rite.

People in various 12-Step recovery groups sometimes insist on using someone who is also in recovery to hear the 5th Step. The reason for that is to help you stay honest. AA does not practice Christianity or Judaism or Hinduism or anything else. They maintain a neutral religion because people have often been abused by religion. Some of them go too far and say "Don't have anything to do with it." Our faith tells us that a priest can do more for you to alleviate guilt and pain than anybody else. I say to people who are in AA and AlAnon, find a priest who is in AA or AlAnon, so they understand what's going on with those issues too. A priest who has no understanding of the issues of alcoholism, and the family issues surrounding them are liable to completely miss the mark of understanding what is going on. But it is no cop-out to go to a priest and make a confession. The priest is the person who has been designated by the community of faith, ordained by the community and God, to speak for both the community and God in absolution and forgiveness. When a priest pronounces absolution and the forgiveness of both God and the community, the person is restored in the sight of both.

"When a confession is heard in a church building, the confessor may sit inside the altar rails or in a place set aside to give greater privacy, and the penitent kneels nearby." A "place set aside for greater privacy" is a confessional booth or some other similar room. "If preferred, the confessor and penitent may sit face to face for a spiritual conference leading to absolution or a declaration of forgiveness." Sometimes priest and parishioner start out in a counseling session and realize after awhile that they have really been in a confession, and say, "Hey, that's what it sounds like," and then move from the counseling to absolution and forgiveness.

"When the penitent has confessed all serious sins troubling the conscience and has given evidence of due contrition, the priest gives such counsel and encouragement as are needed and pronounces absolution." Notice, it does not say "The priest MAY pronounce absolution." It is an instruction as to what happens. The priest does not say, "You did WHAT! There's no way I'll forgive that." Forgiveness is a requirement on the part of the priest. "Before giving absolution, however, the priest may assign to the penitent a psalm, prayer, or hymn to be said, or something to be done, as a sign of penitence and act of thanksgiving."

51

The Seal of Confession

The last paragraph is really important. "The content of a confession is not normally a matter of subsequent discussion. The secrecy of a confession is morally absolute for the confessor (that's the priest or whoever is hearing the confession) and must under no circumstances be broken." Now, that paragraph says that normally you, the penitent, would never bring it up again or make it a topic for subsequent discussion, even in a counseling session. It may be that you would choose to do so because of some later circumstance or continued troubled heart that you had not been able to repair. However, for the confessor, the secrecy is morally absolute, which means that if the priest violates the seal of the confessional, he goes to hell. That's as close to an unforgivable sin as a priest or confessor, hearing a confession, can commit. It is very, very serious.

Until fairly recently, the courts and the legislatures of this country never even thought of challenging the seal of the confessional. There has been some move in that direction in recent years. In Tennessee, for instance, anybody with knowledge of child abuse is subject to prosecution if they fail to notify the authorities. The confessional was included in that knowledge. The Catholic Church took it to court, understandably, and the Episcopal Church filed an *amicus curiae* brief with the court. The law was passed after the Georgian Hills Day Care child abuse case. A lot of people rush into things in the heat of the moment, and afterwards wish they had not been quite so hasty.

What Do You Do?

Now look at the rite. There are two equivalent forms, one starts on 447, one on 449. Normally I meet penitents in my office at a convenient hour. Sometimes we go other places. I turn the phone off, turn on some music to block out outside noises and to minimize any worry about other people accidentally hearing. Doing a confession in the church around the altar means choosing a time when you would not have to worry about traffic, or people stumbling in accidentally. Most people don't want to be seen either, because it is a very private thing. So, normally the office is a better choice.

The confession followed the rubrics on the previous page, seated face to face. Some people find it helpful to have a prayer desk in the office in order to kneel. Kneeling is a posture of penitence; it is your body telling your mind what it ought to be doing. So, it is desirable to have a prayer desk available. The priest says a prayer for the person that their confession will be honest and that they would be blessed by it, and the penitent, in Form I, begins with, "I confess to Almighty God, to his Church, and to you (the priest), that I have sinned by my own fault in thought, word, and deed, in things done and left undone; especially" and then you read your list. It may take an hour, two hours, three hours, or ten minutes. Frequently, if somebody is making a first confession and they are middle aged, it may take awhile because it will lead to some discussion, explanation, and elaboration. A complete confession is not just a list of the Seven Deadly Sins. It goes into specific time, places, things, people, and occurrences, because saying it out loud is important. When complete, the penitent continues, "For these and all other sins which I cannot now remember, I am truly sorry. I pray God to have mercy on me. I firmly intend amendment of life, and I humbly beg forgiveness of God and his Church, and ask you for counsel, direction, and absolution."

It is important to be as thorough as possible and to take seriously the phrase that we are also confessing those sins which we cannot now remember. When we do recall them later we can remember that we have been forgiven. Instead of going back and making a "supplemental" confession we can just dismiss it, say, "Oh, there you are, you were hiding under the baseboard. Now shoo away because you don't belong to me anymore."

The priest offers counsel, direction and comfort, and then pronounces the absolution. While there are two equivalent forms, I like the first one: "Our Lord Jesus Christ, who has left power to his Church to absolve all sinners who truly repent and believe in Him, of His great mercy forgive you all your offenses (the statement is that Christ forgives you your offenses); and by His authority committed to me, I absolve you from all your sins." So God does the forgiving, the priest speaking on behalf of God and the Church then wipes the slate clean. That's what absolution is — the slate is wiped clean, all that stuff is taken away. It is not to be held against you any further either in the community or in the eyes of God.

The priest concludes, "The Lord has put away all your sins." The penitent says, "Thanks be to God." And the priest says, "Go in peace, and pray for me, a sinner."

Another Way

Form II has the comfortable words in it and begins with the priest and penitent praying together for God's mercy. Then the priest says the comfortable words and bids the penitent to make confession. When the penitent is complete, he is asked if he will turn again to Christ as Lord. That is one of the baptismal promises (whenever you sin, will you repent and return to the Lord?). The penitent is then asked "Do you then forgive those who have sinned against you?" We are beginning to move from seeking our own forgiveness to saying also forgiving those who sin against us. The Lord's Prayer is "Forgive us as we have forgiven others." We get the measure of forgiveness that we have given.

The priest then says, "May God in his mercy receive your confession of sorrow and of faith, strengthen you in all goodness, and by the power of the Holy Spirit keep you in eternal life." Following the absolution is a wonderful conclusion, "Now there is rejoicing in heaven; for you were lost, and are found; you were dead, and are now alive in Christ Jesus our Lord. Go in peace. The Lord has put away all your sins." What a WONDERFUL way to end a confession.

Notice that it says "the priest concludes." It does not say "the priest may conclude." Again, the emphasis in reconciliation is on "spiritual counsel and advice to the removal of scruple and doubt, the assurance of pardon, and the strengthening of your faith." The words in both forms for reconciliation underscore the paragraph in the Exhortation and reaffirm that you are the beloved child of God.

The Aftermath

Following the act of reconciliation, the penitent leaves and the priest forgets what was said. One of the graces God gives to priests in ordination is a measure of forgetfulness. The priest does not hold on to somebody else's sins. That would be sick. God has taken them away. They do not belong to the priest and do not stay on his shoulders for having heard them. 98% of the time it leaves the memory. There may be times you bring up something that would remind the priest of the content of your confession, but they don't go around thinking, "Oh, that's the person who did that wicked thing." That honestly just doesn't happen. There are priests who fail. But not taking the risk necessary to receive the grace of absolution leads to grave consequences. If the confessor priest maintains a relationship with you, then you have a lived experience that there is forgiveness with another human being. If I bear my most secret sins to a priest, which I have done, and that priest then chooses to maintain a relationship of friendship with me, and continues to understand me as a priest of the Church and a good Christian person, then I have a lived experience of forgiveness and restoration.

When you are ready, call a priest of the church whom you know to be "discreet and understanding" to hear your confession. That priest may, or may not, be your spiritual director. Make an appointment with the priest for sacramental confession between now and the beginning of Week 10.

The reason for the time span is that the Rite of Reconciliation covers several Steps. Step 6 is "Were entirely ready to have God remove all these defects of character." Step 7 says "Humbly asked him to remove our shortcomings." Once you get ready to make a private confession, be ready to do Steps 5, 6, and 7 because they're all covered in the Rite of Reconciliation. Sequentially what happens is: we confess the sin, we are then ready for God to take the garbage out; so we ask Him to do it.

Get Ready

You have plenty of time to do several things: to screw up your courage to actually make a confession; to be thoroughly ready; and, in case the confessor you choose is unavailable for some time, you have the time to make the appointment. If none of the priests on the list are acceptable to you, then I'll give you a list of other clergy in the diocese.

Some of you may want to add some additional prayers to what you're doing. If you do, I would suggest that you turn to the back of your Prayer Book in the Prayers of Thanksgivings and pick a few. There are some major headings, and you might want to pick one from under each heading and add them to your prayers. For those of you in 12 Step programs, there is a prayer for those who are addicted. For those of you who have teenagers, there is one for young persons. These prayers will not pray for you, however. You can't put the Prayer Book under your pillow and pray by osmosis. What I experience is that when I can't find words for something that is churning around inside of me, I can frequently find the prayer that expresses this churning somewhere in the Prayer Book. Start getting more familiar and friendly with the Book of Common Prayer because it is full of good stuff. Keep your prayer time at a manageable size. You don't have to be a saint yet. The main thing right now is to set a discipline and keep the discipline that's good for you and works for you even if it is not what somebody else has. Good luck during this week on your prayer time.

SPIRITUAL FRIENDSHIP

Step 5: Admitted to God, to ourselves, and to another human being the exact nature of our wrongs.

Discussion Topics

Share experience of prayer time during past week.

How is the Lord calling you to change?

Are you ready to make these changes?

Is the idea of private confession disturbing to you? Hopeful?

Discuss your servant ministry.

Are you satisfied with the spiritual value of your financial pledge?

PRAYER TIME - STEP 5

Theme: Confession

Step 5: Admitted to God, to ourselves, and to another human being the exact nature of our wrongs.

Format
  Preparation (breath prayer, relaxation exercise, etc)
  Read Psalm
  Silence (5 minutes)
  Read Scripture selection
  Silence (5 minutes)
  Personal prayers
  Lord's Prayer
  Collect of the week

Day 1:	Psalm 25	Job 13:20-27
2:	32	Luke 15:11-24
3:	96	Deuteronomy 4:29-31
4:	119:113-120	Deuteronomy 30:1-5
5:	126	Nehemiah 1:5-9
6:	103	James 5:13-20
7:	130	John 7:53-8:11

Collect
    Almighty and everlasting God, You hate nothing You have made and forgive the sins of all who are penitent: Create and make in us new and contrite hearts, that we, worthily lamenting our sins and acknowledging our wretchedness, may obtain of You, the God of all mercy, perfect remission and forgiveness; through Jesus Christ your Son our Lord, who lives and reigns with You and the Holy Spirit, one God, now and forever. Amen.

Ash Wednesday, (BCP, p. 217)

***Make an appointment with a priest for sacramental confession between now
and the beginning of Week 10***

STEP 6:
Were entirely ready to have God remove all these defects of character.

There is a statement in the Alcoholics Anonymous book following the enumeration of these Steps, saying, "We claim progress, not perfection." Being entirely ready sometimes means being entirely ready *with one thing at a time*.

Paul addresses the difficulty of relinquishing our defects in the letter to the Romans. The 7th chapter of Romans is particularly pointed in that regard.

> "I was once alive apart from the law, but when the commandment came, sin revived and I died; the very commandment which promised life proved to be death to me. For sin, finding opportunity in the commandment, deceived me and by it killed me. So that law is holy, and the commandment is holy and just and good. Did that which is good, then, bring death to me? By no means!"

(In other words he was saying the law is not responsible for the sin, although Christians read this and interpret it that way and say, "Well, we shouldn't have paid any attention to the Hebrew scriptures, the 10 Commandments and stuff." Paul says that's not it at all. He says that sin was working death in me through what is good in order that sin might be shown to be sin and through the commandment become sinful beyond measure. Sin sneaks into good things and perverts them. That is how I understand what he is saying there. You start out with a good motivation and then pride takes over. For instance, you do something with selfless motivation, you go help somebody and then you want to pat yourself on the back for doing such a fine job, or ask for thanks, or get your feelings hurt if you don't get thanks.)

> "We know that the law is spiritual; but I am carnal, sold under sin. I do not understand my own actions. For I do not do what I want, but I do the very thing I hate. Now if I do what I do not want, I agree that the law is good. So then it is no longer I that do it, but sin which dwells within me. For I know that nothing good dwells within me, that is, in my flesh. I can will what is right, but I cannot do it. For I do not do the good I want, but the evil I do not want is what I do. Now if I do what I do not want, it is no longer I that do it, but sin which dwells within me."

Taking Personal Responsibility

In the last 20 years we have taken that to the extreme in our culture and said, "Well, I am not responsible." In *We Are Still Married,* Garrison Keillor has a story saying that if Hitler were alive today, he would have an interview with Bryant Gumbel

> "A lot of people still have hard feelings toward you because of that whole Auschwitz thing, you know. What do you say to that? How do you deal with animosity on that level? I mean, personally, you and Eva. Is it rough on your marriage? How do you explain it to your kids?' The former Fuhrer speaks in rapid German and we hear a woman's voice translate: 'Bryant, a person can't look back. I live in the future. People who still carry a grudge from forty— what was it? *Fifty* years ago—that's a tragedy. The stories about genocide are so old and worn out and threadbare and the people who repeat them are—I'm very sorry to have to say this—they're to be pitied. I feel sorry for them. Life is a garden, a summer day, a fragile

butterfly, the smile on the face of a child. Why would I kill millions of people when I myself love life so much?'"

We don't talk about sin anymore. We say, "Well, it wasn't me that did it" and we get an insanity defense, "I was out of my mind when I did that, so I am not responsible." Paul is not saying that. He's not saying "I'm not responsible for what I did." He is saying, "Sin working within me has resulted in my acting in this way, but it was not my choice to be sinful, it was an uncontrollable urge, a compulsion." "For I delight in the law of God, in my inmost self, but I see in my members another law at war with the law of my mind and making me captive."

Work With God

Notice that Step 6 takes the action of both ourselves and God: We become entirely ready, God removes. Paul, in the letter to the Romans, says he is not entirely ready, he wishes he was, he knows better, and yet the sin which clings so closely is hard to get away from and it keeps sneaking back in when he is doing good. It sidles up next to him and then changes his motivations so that he winds up doing the good thing for sinful reasons again. He gets very frustrated with it, and then he has to struggle to turn his actions once more over to God.

Do you remember the painting by Holman Hunt of Christ standing at the ivy covered door knocking? In that picture there is no knob or latch on the outside of the door. The latch and the knob are on the inside. Jesus is always ready to forgive us. One of the collects in the Book of Common Prayer says, "Almighty and everlasting God, you are always more ready to ... give than we ... desire ..." (Proper 22) It makes that point that Christ is always there to give and more willing to give us good things than we are willing to ask for them or to receive them. Christians are not perfect, just forgiven. We are not talking about perfection in spirituality, we are talking about growth.

Forgiveness Precedes Reconciliation

Forgiving is not reconciliation. Forgiving has to do with not allowing sin to cause a permanent rift between us and the other person, or between us and God. It leads to reconciliation. Forgiveness enables us to grow, and it is always being offered. However, we frequently are unwilling to accept it. To be forgiven we must accept and be willing to let go of those things which are our favorite animosities, grudges, and resentments. None of us wants to murder anybody, but sometimes we entertain a murderous desire. Normally healthy people will suppress that impulse to do bodily damage, at least to the extent of actual murder. Normally healthy people will discover that they cannot live with hatred in their being without becoming ill.

We frequently want to reduce the amount of grudge-holding to a level that we can think we can manage, but we don't want to let go of all the grudges. There are some that people deserve to have held against them, right? But what does Jesus say? He said, "You have heard that it was said, thou shall not kill, but I tell you that you should not be angry." "You should not hold grudges" is the way that translates. "You have heard it said that you shall not commit adultery, but I tell you that anyone who looks at another person with lust in his heart has committed adultery already." "All have sinned and fallen short of the glory of God." Peter says, "Lord, how many times must we forgive these people, as many as seven times?" In Hebrew numerology seven is perfection, that is not "one, two, three, four, five, six, seven, that's it." It's "I'll forgive them to perfection." Jesus responds, "No, not seven, but seventy times seven," which is taking perfection to it's *n*th degree. Forgiveness is to be always offered; and we need to learn to offer it and we need to learn to receive it.

Say "Yes" to Good

This Step contributes to our spiritual growth by enabling us to say "yes" to the good that is in us, to goodness and health that will lead us closer to God and closer to the Christian community, and further away from the things that are diseased, whether it is grudge-holding, or lust, or shaving points on a basketball game, or cheating on the income tax, or turning a blind eye when someone is being mugged or raped or robbed. You can bear false witness by telling a lie, and you can bear false witness by not telling the truth.

Be Realistic

Part of our corporate psyche in this country which comes from our Puritan and ultra-Calvinist heritage is the notion of the total depravity of humanity. We feel guilty if we can't find something that we have done wrong. In *We Are Still Married* (pp. 43-45), Keillor talks about the perfect little old blue-headed grandmother who never did anything wrong, who was the most thoughtful person in the world. Somebody said, "She's not all as good as she appears to be." Then he says a mass murderer comes along and people say, "He's not all that bad, not as bad as he seems." You get more forgiveness if you're a really bad person than if you're a really good person. That's part of this sickness in our country that we're fighting against.

If you find that your conscience is clean, don't necessarily assume that it is pride taking over. It could just as easily mean that you haven't done anything good either. Part of it is likely to be denial. Part of it may be "Your sin is so foul and horrible that Christ in His courtesy hasn't chosen to reveal it to you yet." We need the Lord's discernment to find any clarity about what is sinful in us and what's good in us. That is suggested by what Paul says in Romans 7.

It's Not Easy

Becoming ready to relinquish our sinful inclinations is not an easy task. You can't say, "This is bad and I can get rid of it and quit doing it." It is a difficult thing to discern because sin is so seductive. It starts out good, or appears to be good. We choose it because it appears to be good, but then it turns sour somewhere along the line. "Sin enters in," Paul says, and it is so frustrating when it happens. Part of the Spiritual Journey, the Spiritual Quest, is to become more attuned to the first sign that things are starting to go awry. When you have difficulty with temper control, to become aware that the internal conditions are beginning to build up that lead to a point of irrational loss of temper, and to begin to say, wait a minute, let's deal with those little issues right here before they build up to blow the top off the boiler."

Spiritual growth helps to reduce whatever it is that sends us into disfunction, to be able through the grace of God to be able to recognize the conditions as they arise. In marriages, what is it that causes friction between husband and wife? What are the things that build up to it? It becomes even more complicated in subsequent marriages when the old behavior patterns come into the new marriage. For people in second marriages, it becomes very important to do a real house-cleaning and identify within yourself what it was that was friction-causing in the prior relationship.

When we begin to have some spiritual growth, we find ourselves willing to turn our problem attitudes and behavior over to God and to have it taken away. In our relationship with other people, when we seek the Lord's direction, then if we do clash, or get to the point beyond the bounds, we are able to turn around early and say "I'm sorry, my anger didn't belong to you. It came from some other things that are going on in my life and I had not handled well. I am really sorry that I dumped it on you. It really was not the interchange between the two of us that was at fault here." So it becomes easier to make reconciliation and restitution. It becomes easier then to maintain our relationships with God and with one another because we are turning over this character defect, this flaw of behavior patterns, this sinful pattern that we have lived out before. We cannot by force of will change; but we can with the Lord's help.

Jesus Can Do More Than You Can

Some people like to think they can change on their own. I call that the "boot strap theory of salvation," where by your own actions you can reach down by your bootstraps and lift yourself into heaven. We can't save ourselves, but we do have the power to choose to let Christ save us.

Powerlessness in spiritual growth is to recognize that we are powerless over sin. The sooner we accept that the better off we are. From there on, we begin to attach ourselves to the power that is greater than us, the power of the lordship of Jesus Christ. Then we are able, in cooperation with God, to change. It is a cooperative thing. We choose to follow Christ, and we choose to open that door (because the latch is on our side) and to let Christ in. We choose the direction we want to go, but we cannot go there all on our own. When I choose the direction I want to go, my tendency is to say, "Okay, God, I can see the goal now." Then I make the terrible mistake of saying "Now I can make it. I know where you want me to go, so I can make it." But that's wrong. I cannot do it alone.

I know where the Lord wants me to go, I believe I have been given enough vision and clarity to know, and that's to be a parish priest. And I think I know the shape of that calling. To be a good parish priest is not something I can do on my own. It takes Christ working in me to, through my prayer life, to guide and direct me, and through my interaction with parishioners to further hear the word of God as we live together as a parish family. Our choice is to open the door. Christ knocks, we answer. The opening of the door is our responsibility, the spiritual growth is His.

Opening the Door

How do we open the door? One way is by doing what we have been practicing these last 5 or 6 Weeks. We set aside a time for prayer and meditation. We set a listening mood, focus our attention on our relationship with God, and the Lord can speak to us when we are open to Him. We set the appointment, the date with our beloved. The Lord's guidance may not become clear during our prayer time of 5:30 in the morning, or 4:00 in the afternoon, or 11:00 at night, or noon; but once you have opened the door through regular spiritual discipline, the door does not shut again four hours later. It stays open. Guidance may come when the door is nearly shut, when we're not looking, when we turn our back.

Some of the thoughts and directions I find to be the most enlightening, come in hypnogogic moments. Hypnogogic moments occur in the shower, or just before you fall asleep, when you're shaving, or when you are doing something that doesn't take a lot of mental agility, when your body is doing the routine thing and your mind is free and open. Then God can slip in and turn the light on. All of a sudden something you have been wrestling with for weeks or months, finds clarity. I keep a notepad and pencil by the side of the bed to write things down when they come just before sleep. There have been times when I have struggled with a sermon, for instance, and have gotten nowhere, and fretted over it and gone to bed and all of a sudden just as I was falling asleep it all came together; and I have gotten up and done the sermon. It is because the door was left open. That is how the Lord works.

Progress, Not Perfection

As I have already said, we are talking in the Quest about growth, not about perfection. One time Andy Capp's wife said, "What do you want, perfection?" He said, "No, I don't want perfection, just a darn sight less imperfection." That's what spiritual growth is all about; it's getting a darn sight less imperfect. We are not going to find perfection this side of the Jordan. That's God's business in the Kingdom. He probably knows if we attained perfection we would write a book about it, and that would destroy the whole thing with pride. Then we would have to start back at square one and deal with pride again.

In Romans 7 & 8 when Paul is talking about his struggles with striving for perfection it is very illuminating. We struggle with it, we strive for it, we grow in it; but we realize the more we grow, the more there is to grow. Things are better now, but I also have had a glimpse of the Kingdom of God in my spiritual life, but only a glimpse. I still have more growing to do. That taste of the kingdom also raises evangelistic questions in our minds: What about those people who haven't even had a glimpse of the kingdom yet? How do we share the love of God in Christ with them?

Striving is the thing here: Moving towards union with God, continuing to grow, never quitting. Mother Teresa never stopped reading the Scriptures and saying her daily prayers, and she had a darn sight less imperfection than we do. We are here in the world interacting daily with sales people, telephone solicitors, church people; and our opportunity for sin is great. There are more opportunities for sinning than I can take advantage of.

Striving is a key to the Quest. Don't let up just because you are growing. If you let up when we start growing, you stop growing and start sliding backwards again. You either grow or you die; you either get larger or you shrink in your spiritual life.

A Sense of Humor Helps

With time you develop a bit of humility and a sense of humor about your spiritual growth. People who take their spirituality so seriously they never laugh about a prayer they've said or about something that has happened that is weird or odd in their lives, are sick in their spirituality, in their relationship with Christ. Remember, the Hebrew name for God sounds like a chortle, a belly laugh: Yahweh. The English translation of Yahweh is "I am who I am," which seems to me to be more a humorous evasion than a name. So the really serious Christians need to be prodded a little bit to laugh at themselves.

A new Christian should never put on the vestry because they are already narrowly focused with the seriousness of their commitment. If you put them on the vestry it will kill them, because if you can't laugh at the vestry, you will be in serious trouble in about two meetings. There have been times when we have spent two hours talking about a $10 expenditure and then voted on a $130,000 budget in 30 seconds. That's pretty funny. Vestries frequently have a really distorted sense of priorities; so people with a sense of humor about their own position before God need to be on the vestry.

"They're Back"

There are some things that no matter how many times we turn them over to the Lord they keep sneaking up and coming back to us. It's like taking your dog out to the country and leaving it on a farm. Before you get home it's already back at the house, sitting on the porch waiting for you. I think a sense of humor about it at that point becomes really important. You need to be able to say, "I know it's here, Lord. Is this the thorn in the flesh that You have for me? Is this here to afflict me and to remind me that I have to depend upon You alone? If so, all right, let me keep an eye on this clinging sin. If I keep an eye on it, then it has less of a chance to bite me."

There is a prayer of thanksgiving in the back of the Prayer Book that has this line, "We thank you also for those disappointments and failures that lead us to acknowledge our dependence on you alone." The "sin that clings so closely" is addressed by that line. Since I have struggled with it for years, and am not able to let go of it, let me be grateful that it reminds me that I am not God, that I am dependent upon Him not just to take away the things that are sinful in my life, but also to acknowledge that He is the one in control, and His purposes are greater than mine.

When you lock an abiding sin in the closet of denial, though, it grows. So developing a sense of humor about such things is really important. Being able to laugh at ourselves and say "Oh, you'll never guess what I did—again!" Humor takes away a great deal of the power of the sin. It is an acknowledgment that we are not choosing to do sin, that it is a compulsion controlling us. When we recognize the compulsion, very often it is gone. When we say "I am going to control it, it's not a compulsion, it's not something I HAVE to do, I can control it," then we've lost. If we say, "Okay, I can't control this, so I am going to get out of its way and let it blow by," the Lord comes to our help. Again, we are the ones who open the door to Christ, but He is the one who enters our souls to restore us to health.

THE SERENITY PRAYER

God, grant me the serenity
to accept the things I cannot change;
the courage to change the things I can;
and the wisdom to know the difference.

SPIRITUAL FRIENDSHIP

Step 6: Were entirely ready to have God remove all these defects of character.

Discussion Topics

 Share experience of prayer time during past week
 How is the Lord calling you to change?
 Are you ready to make these changes?
 Have you asked the Lord to help you change?
 How are the other elements of the Quest helping you become ready? Corporate worship?
  Private worship? Reading? Working? Giving? Direction? Friendship?

PRAYER TIME - STEP 6

Theme: Readiness for Change

Step 6: Were entirely ready to have God remove all these defects of character.

Format
Preparation (breath prayer, relaxation exercise, etc.)
Read Psalm
Silence (5 minutes)
Read Scripture selection
Silence (5 minutes)
Personal prayers
Lord's Prayer
Collect of the week

Day 1:	Psalm 30	Luke 18:10-14
2:	31	John 8:31-36
3:	119:1-8	John 13:3-10b
4:	121	Micah 7:7-9
5:	125	II Corinthians 7:9-11
6:	139	James 4:7-10
7:	144	Mark 5:25-34

Collect
O God, whose glory it is always to have mercy: Be gracious to all who have gone astray from Your ways, and bring them again with penitent hearts and steadfast faith to embrace and hold fast the unchangeable truth of Your Word, Jesus Christ your Son; who with You and the Holy Spirit lives and reigns, one God, for ever and ever. Amen.

Second Sunday in Lent, (BCP, p. 218)

STEP 7:
Humbly asked God to remove our shortcomings.

In Step 7 we continue with the process of moving from a very closed person, relative to God and to others, towards finally coming into union with God and the world around us. It begins with the moral inventory and grows through openly admitting our wrongs to another person, specifically a priest, to God and to ourselves. Admitting them to ourselves is sometimes the hardest part, and that accounts for much of the resistance to actually doing the moral inventory.

Once we have admitted to ourselves the contents of our secret places, we discover things were not as bad as we thought. It's like the shadows in the dark. When we see our sins in the full light of day, they're not as big and scary as we thought they were.

We have come from admitting to God, ourselves, and another human being the exact nature of our wrongs to a willingness to let God take them away, to asking him to do so. It's a logical progression, and a necessary one. We can't get to the stage of asking God to take things away if we are not ready; and we can't be ready until we have owned up to what is there; and we can't own up to it until we have taken inventory to find out what's there.

A Word From Our Sponsor

In asking God to take away our shortcomings, the virtue of humility really begins to grow. In the 18th chapter of St. Luke's Gospel, Jesus told this parable to some who trusted in themselves that they were righteous and who despised others:

> "Two men went up into the temple to pray, one a Pharisee and the other a tax collector. The Pharisee stood and prayed thus with himself, 'God, I thank thee that I am not like other men, extortioners, unjust, adulterers, or even like this tax collector. I fast twice a week, I give tithes of all that I get.' But the tax collector, standing far off, would not even lift up his eyes to heaven, but beat his breast, saying, 'God, be merciful to me a sinner!' I tell you, this man went down to his house justified rather than the other; for every one who exalts himself will be humbled, but he who humbles himself will be exalted."

At first glance, there is not a whole lot wrong with the Pharisee's position; he's grateful to God that he has been able to live a righteous life, he is grateful to God that he has been able to observe Torah, he's grateful that, as a result of his wealth, he doesn't have to traffic with sinners, to have commercial intercourse with people who are unclean or unkind or unrighteous. The problem is in his comparison of himself with others rather than in his acknowledgment of his own blessings. That is a danger that we run into. It takes a humble person to say, "God, I am really grateful for what I have."

In Luke 17:7-10, Jesus tells the story of the steward. When the master of the house comes home, he doesn't say to the servant, "Well, you've had a hard day, why don't you sit here while I fix your dinner." Instead he says to the servant, "Fix me dinner, and afterwards you can have your own and rest." Jesus makes the point, when we have done all that is required, our proper posture is to say, "Lord, we are not worthy of praise, we've only done what was asked."

In the parable of the Pharisee and the Publican, Jesus is saying that a prayer of thanksgiving which is really a put down of somebody else is missing the point. We are called to look at ourselves and the blessings we have received and then to use them in doing the Lord's work.

Willingness

To develop humility in the place of pride and self-righteousness, we must be able to see and willing to admit our own character defects, our own sinfulness. We make the admission not to be guilty, to feel bad about ourselves, to be blamed for the evils of the world, or to be condemned to hell for all the terrible things we've done. The willingness to see and to admit our character defects, our faults, our sins in life is necessary in order that we may find forgiveness, in order that we may have those defects, those blotches on our record, on our lives, removed. The reason the light is shown in the darkness is so that even the corners will be exposed to light. If we keep a wound covered up in the darkness, it will heal more slowly. Wounds need to be exposed to the sunlight to heal better. So we're exposing these wounds to the sunlight, not so that we can say, "I guess we're really going to hell after all," but so that our Lord can heal our sickness, remove our sins, and give us salvation.

A new perspective is necessary, a perspective that things that build character are to be sought after. The challenges toughen us. The ones that result in success build character. If the ones that result in failure are turned over to God then we can give thanks for those failures that lead us to acknowledge our dependence on God alone. Our successes and our failures, those strife-filled times, can be character building, and can strengthen us for spiritual growth.

A Need for Discipline

A perspective that seeks good in the midst of adversity requires a willingness to place spiritual matters first in our lives. The Spiritual Quest is to place the relationship with our Lord above all other relationships. Converting that willingness to reality involves work and discipline. Paul points out that people in races don't enter a race without practicing, without working up to it. They first wear their bodies out running and running and running. A lot of pain comes to muscles when we haven't used them before. Sometimes it is very, very difficult to even get up out of the bed and move those sore, stiff muscles. Sometimes they have to be massaged and rubbed down with liniment. If we are going to run the race we have to keep it up until the muscles don't hurt any more, until they're tough and wiry and strong. When they're stronger, we're happier. Our heart beats fewer times; it beats stronger; it moves the blood around better; our blood pressure goes down; excess weight comes off.

Paul uses the analogy of a contest to describe the spiritual life. We have to exercise it; we have to work. When it hurts, when it makes the spiritual muscles sore, then that is the sign that we are getting somewhere. The pain marks the break-through point, the coming of the second wind—if we'll just push on through. Spiritual growth in the middle of the 12 Steps is pushing us to make a decision, to choose to exercise our spirituality in ways we have not done before.

Humility is an indispensable element here. If we're not humble, we get cocky, and when we get cocky, we don't work as hard because we think we are better than everybody else.

The parable of the Pharisee and the Publican in Luke 18 makes the point that honesty and morality are not the same thing as humility. The Pharisee in the story is honest and moral, but like a lot of honest, moral people he is anything but humble. Jesus lifts up humility over honesty and morality. Our Lord's friends and disciples were a lot of humble people, but they were not necessarily either honest or moral, at least before they responded to his call to follow him. Step 7 speaks first of humility—"Humbly asked him to remove our shortcomings." A big dose of surrender is also involved here.

Surrender

If we are going to ask God to take something away, then we are surrendering that to him. Three incidents of surrender will illustrate the point. Two are personal experiences in which surrender was absolutely necessary in order for me to live. The first one was in Vietnam. I was sitting on the ground with a loaded Smith and Wesson .38 Combat Masterpiece. However, I was surrounded by 50 to 100 people, four of whom had automatic rifles. Fighting, at that point, was a dumb choice. Surrender offered the only opportunity for survival. If I had chosen to fight, I would have been killed. If I surrendered, it could have gone either way. I was not sure how it would go, but I knew that the only chance I had was to surrender, so I surrendered. It turned out well.

The same year, I surrendered to what I understood to be a call to ordained ministry. I had first felt this "call" when I was fifteen, but it frightened me. In spite of throwing myself into other pursuits, a strong sense of call returned about every two years. While I enjoyed some notable success, particularly as an Air Force navigator, there was a lingering sense of emptiness that could not be filled by anything other than God. When I finally made the decision to seek ordination, some impossibly blocked doors fell open before me. Surrender to God's call to Holy Orders opened up to me a way of freedom and peace even more significant than the opening of the cells of the Hanoi Hilton.

Another kind of surrender is to the surgeon's knife. A person with a malignancy has a choice: refuse surgery and die; or have surgery and possibly die anyway. The only chance he has to live is to have the surgery, have the cancer removed, take the radiation or chemotherapy intended to prolong life. To refuse the surgery, to fight it alone, is a choice for death. To surrender to surgery opens up the possibility for life.

Surrender to Christ does not mean that you will live forever in this life and in this body. It does not mean that a fortune cookie will come true. It does not mean that everybody is going to fall in love with you and put you on a pedestal or anything like that. Refusal to surrender does guaranty that we will not grow spiritually. Surrender opens the possibility of spiritual growth, and my experience says that it is a really strong possibility. Refusal simply means that we are not going to grow.

Once we've made the choice to have Christ as our Lord and Savior, to grow into union with God, then there are some things that we can do to facilitate that union. As with any relationship, there is always going to be a quality of risk involved. You can always get hurt, sometimes by the meanness of other people, sometimes by happenstance, sometimes by the problems that have been created by human industry. But surrender also opens up the possibility for something good. You never know what God is going to give back until you have given him everything.

A great deal of what we are is what God intends for us to be. Well, I don't know about you, but I don't think my judgment is insightful enough to know with absolute certainty what it is about me that God put there, and what it is about me that I put there, and what it is about me that my upbringing and my environment and my experiences in life put there. If we can surrender everything to God, what Christ put in us comes back, fertilized and growing; and what we put in ourselves that is unhelpful, unhealthy, or destructive doesn't come back, unless we reach out and take it back. The result of following through, of recognition of who we are before God, and asking for His mercy is that we grow in spiritual depth and understanding. The publican knows that he has let God down; and as he comes in to make his prayers, he doesn't raise his eyes at all, he doesn't stand with his eyes to heaven. He is so well aware of his own failure that he casts his eyes down and asks for mercy.

We have not built the Kingdom of God. At best we have done what we have been called to do. That is nothing to be terribly ashamed of. Doing our duty is not a shameful thing. One would hope that we would do it cheerfully because we really want to and because we love the Lord, but there's something to be said for doing it even when we don't feel like it. The results of all this can lead to peace of mind and serenity.

Peace of mind comes when we experience humility in a different way. Whereas at one time we looked at humility as being forced-fed humble pie, having our faults stuffed down our throats, our blunders broadcast on the evening news, our children parading them before us to teach us a lesson that we're not as great as we thought.

Humility Leads to Serenity

Our understanding changes from that kind of humiliation to a humility that is a nourishing ingredient adding to serenity. If I am better than everybody else, if I know more than anybody else, then I have a responsibility to save the world. I have to rescue the kids; I have to rescue the parishioners; I have to go out when the sexton doesn't mow the grass and mow it myself; I have to fix something that's broken because I am tired of looking at it and because nobody else is smart enough to do it or intelligent enough or cares enough about it. That is a terrible burden. Humility teaches me to align my priorities with God's priorities, to see myself as part of a larger group—not the rescuer, not the messiah, not the savior of the world, but a member of the body of Christ.

You can almost feel the presence of a truly humble person, just like you can feel a truly arrogant person or a truly angry person. An angry person makes the hair on the back of my neck stand up; an arrogant person makes my shoulders stiff; and a truly humble person brings a kind of a peace to a room. There is a peace that surrounds them. When they are around, we are drawn to them.

Commitment

Peace and serenity is a gift of God, but one which requires our long term commitment to fully receive. This spiritual growth is no easy program. The 12 Steps are pretty simple; you can tick them off on your fingers to know what you're supposed to do; but doing them is like running a race, like preparing your muscles. As a result of the Quest our weaknesses are turned into strength, and our liabilities into assets. Whereas we started our Spiritual Quest admitting that we are without power over cosmic, cultural, and personal sin and evil, and that we cannot control the universe around us, as we grow we discover there's a great deal of power and strength available to us. God made us and loves us and will strengthen us. As we grow humility reminds us that the power is not ours alone, it is our partnership with our Lord Jesus Christ that gives us the strength to face the trials of life.

Paul prayed to God to take his "thorn in the flesh" away from him, but he didn't. So Paul turned that liability into an asset. He said, "Look, here I am, I'm ugly, I'm irascible, but God is continuing to take the word, the gospel of Jesus Christ to the world through me." That is a miracle. In all of Paul's weakness, God's strength shines through. It gave Paul the ability to walk into Nero's court and stand at the stake without fear and to be burned alive for his devotion to his Lord.

A New Understanding of God

As our lives grow with spiritual assets, one of the changes we experience is our attitude towards God. A spiritually immature person may see God as a kind of pinch-hitter. When we are behind 6 to 0 and it's the ninth inning, we call him in off the bench and say "Okay, God, I'm in a real bad mess, You've got to come fix it." We call him in like a pinch-hitter, and as soon as the game is won, we say "Okay, You can go to the showers."

Another immature idea of God is "Maximum Bob." Maximum Bob was the nickname of the judge in the Jim and Tammy Bakker trial. God is Maximum Bob. If we screw up he's going to give us a sentence for eternity. We have to try to appease him by asking for favors and convincing him with extenuating circumstances so maybe we'll get off with 45 years and half a million dollar fine, an extra millennium or two in purgatory before we get to go to heaven, or something like that. (Bakker's attorney wanted as his punishment to send old Bakker back to the PTL Club to restore the thing and build it back up. The fox ate half the chickens, but if you let him go back in the chicken house, he'll put them back.) Those are just two ideas of God held by spiritually immature people.

A more mature idea is to see God as a close and intimate friend, someone we can just talk with naturally. Our prayers lose Elizabethan English and take on 20th Century American—"down and out and put out and at the end of the day" kind of language. A close and intimate friend is a couple of things. He heals us in our infirmities, but he also confronts us in our hardness of heart. The close friend is the one who will pat us on the back when we're hurt and say it will be better. But when we are being a real turkey, the close friend will say "Hey, what are you talking about? You ought to be ashamed of yourself. Now get off your old pity pot and get on with life." That is more my idea of God.

God will chastise. The Bible says a father doesn't punish or discipline somebody else's children. So God disciplines us. The Lord shows our hardness of heart to us in ways that we can change and be willing to turn that over to Him. With time and effort and really working our spiritual program, humility will change from a bitter pill to a happy ingredient of a joyful life, and will help us to move out from ourselves and towards others, and move out from ourselves and towards God.

It is humility that says, "I need you in my life, because without my connection with you I will be diminished, and I don't choose to be diminished. I need God in my life because without God in my life I would be diminished, I would not be as full as I could be otherwise."

Jacob Wrestles with God

There's a funny thing about us, and it's been going on forever. In the 33rd chapter of Genesis we get the story of Jacob coming home. We all know that Jacob was a twin of Esau. Esau was born first, but Jacob was grasping Esau's heel. As they go through life Jacob was always trying to steal the birthright from Esau, even though God had promised it to Jacob. In the 33rd chapter of Genesis Jacob is coming home. He finally decided to face Esau, but he is not so courageous and he surely is not humble. He has two wives, Leah and Rachel. He was tricked by Laban into marrying Leah. He wanted Rachel. Leah had bad eyes. The veil was over them at the wedding and when they took the veil off he said, "Uh oh." He had to work another seven years to get Rachel. Jacob is concerned that Esau is still pretty angry with him, so what does he do? He separates the wives' families, and he sends Leah on ahead, because he figures that if Esau is so mad he is going to destroy his family he can have Leah and her children. Jacob is not a nice person.

As he is waiting for Esau, Jacob has his dream of the ladder in which he struggled with God. While the story says Jacob prevailed over God, Jacob had his name changed. In the Old Testament, when God changed somebody's name, God took possession of that person. Remember the way Adam and Eve took possession of the animals was by naming them. God said, "What do you think that ought to be called?" "Dog. Cow." In the naming, Adam took possession of the animals as a custodian. That is what we do with our children. We are all in a panic to name our children. They are incomplete until they are named. We don't leave them nameless until they make up their own mind about what they want to be called. So when God changes a name, God takes control. He changed Jacob into Israel, which means "Contended with God." He also put Jacob's hip out of joint so that he has to limp for the rest of his life to remind him just who is in control.

We Wrestle with God

We contend with God, too. We continue in that process of being Israel. If you're going to grow into union with God, part of what you're going to do is struggle. We struggle and we gain humility a little bit at a time. Jacob became Israel a little bit at a time. It took a long time for God to work His purposes out with him, and it's going to take Him a long time with us. It took Him a hundred years to work his purposes out with Abraham and Sarah before they could have a baby. It takes time, but it will happen; we will change.

It also takes a little courage. Courage is not the absence of fear; it is acting in the face of fear, knowing you have fears, not denying them, but keeping them out where you can see them and moving on and doing what you are called to do, whether it's fighting a war, having children, getting married, joining a church, singing in the choir, or going to work every day. You act anyway. If you need to do it, you do it. Slowly the fears begin to subside, and slowly we're changed into this new being that Christ would have us to be.

SPIRITUAL FRIENDSHIP
Step 7: Humbly asked Him to remove our shortcomings.

Discussion Topics
Share experience of prayer time during past week.
How is the Lord calling you to change?
Have you asked the Lord to help you change?
Are you estranged from anyone? What is it like?
Do you have some shortcomings you want your Spiritual Friend to pray about?
What are they?
Have you made an appointment for a confession? If not, why not?

PRAYER TIME - STEP 7

Theme: Request for Change

Step 7: Humbly asked him to remove our shortcomings.

Format

    Preparation (breath prayer, relaxation exercise, etc.)
    Read Psalm
    Silence (5 minutes)
    Read Scripture selection
    Silence (5 minutes)
    Personal prayers
    Lord's Prayer
    Collect of the week

Day 1:	Psalm 6	I John 1:8-10
2:	49	Matthew 6:5-8
3:	51	Acts 26:15-17
4:	65	Ephesians 4:14-16
5:	103	II Thessalonians 2:13-17
6:	116	Matthew 21:18-22
7:	119:33-40	Galatians 6:14-16

Collect

    Stir up your power, O Lord, and with great might come among us; and, because we are sorely hindered by our sins, let Your bountiful grace and mercy speedily help and deliver us; through Jesus Christ your Son our Lord, who lives and reigns with You and the Holy Spirit, one God, now and for ever. Amen.

Third Sunday of Advent, (BCP, p. 212)

STEP 8:

Made a list of all persons we had harmed and became willing to make amends to them all.

In the Book of Common Prayer there is a prayer for our enemies that is helpful as we begin the next three steps. In Step 8 of the Spiritual Quest we make a list of all persons we have harmed and become willing to make amends to them all.

Forgiveness is something you do that requires nobody else's participation. Your forgiveness of other people is a gift to them. It is also one you give to yourself because refusal to forgive creates an acid in our souls that eats us spiritually and, in some cases, physically. Grudge-bearing can lead to stresses that result in everything from ulcers to colitis, to heart attack, to high blood pressure, to cancer.

When we start taking Steps 8, 9 & 10, we are moving towards reconciliation, which is one Step beyond forgiveness. Step 8 is an inventory of damages done to others; Step 9 is an action Step to repair the damages that we have caused; and Step 10 is a Step of daily maintenance and repair.

"An Ounce of Prevention. . ."

In the 1960's, the Southern Railway System was the only railroad in the country that made money. All the other railroads, in order to keep a high volume of cars in service, ran trains more frequently and cut down on maintenance. They quickly became less reliable in their delivery because the maintenance was poor. Southern Railway cut down on the frequency of their trains in order to maintain them better, and they were able to get the freight to market more quickly and reliably. Consequently, they were given more business and made more money. In more recent years we have witnessed the results of not doing regular preventative maintenance on bridges. They fall down and people die.

The same thing occurs in our relationships with others. These next three Steps have to do with interpersonal relationships. We have repaired and improved our relationship with our Lord in Steps 2 through 7, but that is not enough. We also have to actively work on our relationships with other people.

Resistance

As with Steps 4, 5 & 6, a great deal of resistance develops as we continue to grow spiritually. Step 4 was just making a list, but it was still scary. We didn't like to do Step 4 partly because we knew Step 5 was coming up, but also in part because we were afraid there was something inside our lives that would destroy us if we ever acknowledged its presence.

Step 8 presents us with similar fears. There are some fractured relationships with family members, friends, and others, some of whom may not even know we offended or injured them. As we consider what we are going to do with the list, the obstacles begin to build.

Reluctance to Forgive

The first obstacle is likely to be a reluctance to forgive. You have said or heard somebody else say, "I can never forgive them for what they did to me. They cheated me, they lied to me, they hurt me, they stole something from me." That focuses on a wrong done to us rather than the other way around. We are truly powerless over the actions of others; but we do not have to add to the injury done by them by holding grudges. Step 8 focuses on what we have done without the distraction of the wrongs of others. Set aside the offenses that have been laid upon you. Sort the complex of strained, damaged, or broken relationships and try to discern which faults are yours and which ones are someone else's. Lay aside other's wrongs through honest forgiveness and accept responsibility for your own. So often people assume either that the other person was 100% at fault or that we were 100% at fault. In reality, it is a mixture. These Steps will help separate the actions of various people so that you can begin to deal with what belongs to you in a realistic fashion.

If you remember, our Lord tells us, "If you come to the altar to make your offering to Almighty God, and you get there with your offering and remember that you have anything at all against your brother, leave your offering where it is, go, be reconciled first, and then come and make your offering to God." He doesn't say take your offering with you and go, because God knows we would probably keep the offering and not be reconciled either. He also doesn't say make your offering to God and then go, because we would say our general confession to God, make our offering, and say, "Well, I am now redeemed, and I don't have to do anything. The Lord has taken away my sin, and I don't have to be reconciled because that's already been done in some mystical way." Well, that's not what Jesus said.

Remember the Lord's Prayer: "Forgive us our sins as we forgive those who sin against us." The order is: we are forgiven as we forgive; God forgives us as we forgive others. So if we want to be forgiven, we must first give it. Remember, too, the story Jesus told about the speck in the other person's eye and the log in your own. Of course, if you have a speck in your eye it feels like a log. It might not be a giant and horrible sin that is in your eye, but it will gnaw at you as though you had a limb stuck in there, aggravating and irritating. A grain of sand or an eyelash will do it to you. It may not be big, but if we are to see clearly, we need to be honest about what is stuck in our own eyes and get it out and get rid of it. Then we can find forgiveness, and can move forward in our spiritual quest. Honest personal evaluation also makes the other person's fault look a lot smaller and enables us to understand their actions and motivations.

By this point in the steps of the Quest, the logical movement should be clear. The order is that we have sought forgiveness from God and the church for the wrong we have done. If we have done Steps 5, 6 and 7 thoroughly, by the time we get to Step 8 our own obstacles to grace will be much reduced. We will be ready to move now from forgiveness to reconciliation because we will have experienced the forgiveness that comes with the laying on of hands and the words of absolution in confession.

Unwillingness to Admit Our Wrongs

The obstacle in our spiritual path now is the unwillingness to admit our wrongs to the people we have harmed. People may not be aware of some things we have done. Making amends to them could be harmful to them. Out of pastoral concerns for them, we may not be able to make amends.

Diversion

Another obstacle is a tendency toward diversion. This form of non-admission says, "When I did that I was really hurting myself. When I cheated on that exam, I was really hurting me. When I shaved on my income taxes, it was just me that I was really hurting; or I lost my integrity when I did that, and so I really didn't hurt anybody else, just myself." It sounds like self-justification and it is a way of side-stepping the work of eventually moving towards reconciliation.

These obstacles prevent us from doing Step 8 because we know Step 9 comes next. Take them in order. First, make the list. Then plan how to act on the list.

Denial

Another obstacle is purposeful forgetting, or denial. Words and actions could be recorded; but a person will say "you misunderstood; I didn't really mean that." Whether it is outright denial or reinterpretation of facts, it is purposeful forgetting; that is to say "I didn't really do what I really did do."

We struggle with these things as we grow spiritually because we are afraid of what will happen to already strained relationships. Some estrangements occur. The pain has been buried for a long time and covered over by a veneer of politeness. We say, "All that's been settled. See how well we get along now."

When Saigon fell in 1976, the Vietnam generation stopped talking about the differences between those who fought in and supported the war and those who resisted the war or protested against it. It was over now; Saigon had finally fallen; and there was one Vietnam again. So we just stopped talking about the war for 10 years. There was a polite veneer simulating reconciliation, but the country was not getting well. We were acting more and more strangely in foreign relations. As a corporate entity the nation was getting sicker until the fall of 1982. With the dedication of the Vietnam Veterans Memorial in Washington, D.C., the wounds were reopened. Some people said it looked like an ugly scar, a black cut in the mall. In a way that is what it was, and in a way it did open the wounds and a lot of infection came out from underneath and rose to the surface. Since 1982 we have been dealing with our estrangement; we have been getting better; we are being healed as a people.

Reconciliation Becomes Possible

The same process occurs on the individual level. When we finally deal directly and honestly with estrangements, reconciliation becomes possible. If we do not deal with estrangements, they will never get better. But if we face them directly, they have a chance to heal. There are no guarantees; it may stay the same, it may even for the moment get a little worse, but there will not be any hope for growth and reconciliation as long as we keep things covered up, as long as we as Christian people do not make an attempt to go to the ones from whom we are estranged and say, "Within this relationship this is how I was at fault."

Possible Rejection

A fear is they will say "Yes, you were at fault, you were wrong, and I never want to see you again." Well, that is a problem. Reconciliation will not be effected when that happens, at least not right away. You may have somebody blow up in your face; you may get a stunned look that says "I don't remember that," and you may get relief that says "That was wonderful," and you may get written up in *Reader's Digest*.

Every once in awhile you read an article in *Reader's Digest* or *Guidepost* or something else, about somebody who stole a lawnmower from somebody's garage 50 years ago. Then, in an attempt to make amends, they come back to the old neighborhood, find the person they stole it from and buy them a brand new Lawn Boy. They say, "I took this and I'm sorry, here's the restitution." We read it and think it is wonderful and heartwarming to see that somebody finally, after a long of span of years, has relieved their conscience and has made restitution and has sought reconciliation.

A Quiet Conscience

That is what we are after here, to quiet our conscience so that we can live a calm, peaceable life within our own selves. The whole world may be in utter chaos, but at least within ourselves there will be a center of serenity and quietness where we can be at peace and know that God is with us and God loves us.

All of this means that we have to be, as with Step 4, exhaustive in our search. Go back as early as you can remember. List everything you can think of. Go back and forth in time. When you write down something recent you may be reminded of a situation when you were younger, or *vice versa*.

Questions

Questions will naturally arrive about amendments. "Can I repair this? Is it possible?" Don't worry about that yet, that's the next Step. You may not be able to repair some of the damages. Some people may be dead. An acquaintance said that he had gone to the graves of his grandparents because there were some things he needed to seek forgiveness for from them. He said what he had to say there at their graves. We believe that the Church Triumphant is in communication with the Church Militant. For him there was something powerfully symbolic about going to that place and making his apology.

That kind of reconciliation also occurs at the Vietnam Veterans Memorial in Washington because the names are on the Wall as a kind of tombstone. By touching the names, there is some communication there that really occurs.

Impossible Repairs

Some of your estrangements may be with people who have long since gone to meet their Maker. You can't deal with them eyeball to eyeball, but there may be some other way to be reconciled. At other times you cannot repair the damages. If you wrecked somebody's car in a parking lot 30 years ago, you probably cannot go back and repair it now.

It may not be possible to do anything with some damages in real physical terms, but you can begin to make some response in spiritual terms. You may need to delay some of the repairs because the timing isn't right for the other person, because time and distance have separated you from the possibility of doing it right now, because the other person is ill and you do not want to go in to their sick room and bring up unpleasant memories.

Action is Necessary

Sooner or later, though, action is necessary. If you do not deal with the past, the hurts will continue to fester. Like a growth under the skin or inside the body, if you ignore it, it will not go away; it will get bigger and bigger. It may sit there in a little knot and take up space; it may grow like a cancer or boil and cause great damage to you. These steps are for self-preservation and spiritual growth. That is why we are here.

Benefits

There are some benefits, some really good benefits to thorough amendment-making. One is deepened insight into who you are and into who God is. We get that insight as we did with Steps 4, 5, 6, and 7, through thorough examination and thorough consideration of who we are. Most of us discover that when we have really been thoroughly honest and really as objective as any of us can be, we are not as bad as we had thought we were going to be. We are our own worst judges. We get a really positive insight that while we have offended others, we have not been absolutely callous or wicked or evil. By thoroughness of examination and by the resultant insight, we gain self-knowledge, and in turn, the power of the Lord is unleashed as we find honesty growing in our lives. As a result we begin to understand better why we acted the way we did; and when we understand the emotions and motives behind the actions, then we have more options for what we are going to do in the future. We can behave differently next time.

People in associated 12 Step recovery programs like AlAnon, AlaTeens, or ACOA, or what have you, know that a lot of behavior is based upon old ways of dealing with the world that are conditioned by relationships with people who were sick. As the person gets healthier in a 12 Step program, he or she finds more positive options for ways of living life. That is also central to the Quest. By looking at ourselves, by scrutinizing the action, the emotion, and the relationship between the emotion and the action, then we can make different choices in the future.

A common thing that happens to people, if a beloved person is away—whether that beloved is a child, or a spouse, or a girl friend or boy friend—if we don't know where they are, we get very fearful. Curfew is missed; we don't know where they are. Fear grows up inside us. Now fear is a lot like anger. The emotional content is almost indistinguishable. When we are finally reunited with that person about whose safety we were frantic, we blow up on them; we chew them out, yell at them, scream at them, accuse them of all kinds of dastardly deeds, ground them for the rest of their natural life. It comes out as anger.

If we understand that fear and anger feel the same, then we can, with the power of the Holy Spirit, on occasion be able to stop and say, "Listen, I'm very frightened. I missed you, I was worried about your safety, I was worried about your health, all kinds of gremlins crept in there and I imagined that you had been abducted, beheaded, raped, robbed, mugged and all that sort of stuff. I am very relieved that you're safe." That is honest. Instead of "You really hacked me off," we have a choice now of saying to that person that "I love you very much and I was worried about you. I am glad you are safe." Then you can sit down and reasonably say, "Now next time there is this set of circumstances, what can we do to alleviate my anxiety? I need you to respond to me because I am anxious." Rather than taking a negative or irrational tack, we can choose a positive course.

Harm to Others

There are a lot of ways in which we do harm to others. Harm is the result of instincts in collision which cause physical, mental, emotional, or spiritual damage to people. When we collide with another, we cause physical, mental, emotional, or spiritual damage. Our anger arouses the anger in other people. Nobody MAKES me mad, but my angry response comes from an angry confrontation. I am the victim of my emotions, piqued by yours. Lying deprives other people of their goods or of emotional security. A lie is a constructed false reality, and if someone buys into my lie, they are buying into something that is unreal and it will warp their sense of security. If they believe the lie then other things that are concrete and truly real become unreal. It all gets very confusing, and peace of mind disappears.

Lying, cheating, and stealing are the big three that we can all tag because of the harm they cause, but there are a lot of subtle ones, too. The subtle ones are the ones we need to look at very carefully. For instance, miserliness, just plain being stingy, can hurt others, because it breaks or strains relationships as does being irresponsible or callous or cold to others. Sometimes, particularly in a church where people enjoy one another's company, we are being so warm with the people we like that we are being totally cold and callous to the people that walk in the front door looking for a friend. We may not know it, but we do damage to such people. Nobody walks in the front door of a church by accident. There is no reason to be here except to worship God. On Sunday morning people come in looking for God and looking for God's people, and if they don't find it, they are hurt. Churches need to look at their treatment of visitors for their own spiritual growth and health, to see how it is that they have been cold and callous, whether wittingly or unwittingly.

Being irritable, impatient, and humorless are subtle ways of hurting and sapping people's strength. Humorlessness about your faith is particularly damaging. God is a God of humor. People who frown about their faith are not worshiping the God that I know. God made the Leviathan just for the fun of it. The Bible pictures God as a God who enjoys his creation and makes some things just for fun. God could have made human beings to be self-reproductive like an amoeba; but he wanted us to have a little fun reproducing so he made us a different way. God gave us a sense of humor and he expects us to use it in relationship with Him as well as in our relationship with others.

Another way in which we do harm is by giving all of our attention to one person and none of it to another. In families we know the forgotten child, and the one who gets all the attention. Of course, the quiet people frequently don't get any attention—the squeaky wheel gets the grease. We need to look at that. How do we, as Christian people, give God's love across the board and how do we withhold it?

Always wanting our own way, being dominating and demanding, hurts others, because it doesn't allow other people to be fulfilled. That's the skunk side of a personality. The turtle side is being depressed and self-pitying and always wanting attention because "I'm just such a poor, pitiful person and golly, gee whiz, I know why nobody wants to be around me—shucks, I am just no fun to be around." Turtles do more damage than skunks. Skunks will start a good fight and you can duke it out with them. You can't fight with turtles because it just confirms what they are saying. So turtles can really manipulate the dickens out of anyone, and literally steal the emotional strength of everybody around them.

Maintain a Sense of Humor

As we make this list it is important to not be real extreme in our judgment, but to maintain a sense of humor. Do not condemn either yourself or other people in this process. The purpose of this list is *not* so we can say, "My gosh, look how many people's lives I've damaged" or to say, "You know I've hurt these people a little bit but they have really beaten up on me." That is not the purpose of Step 8. This Step helps us to recognize that we are indeed people who have made errors, but also to recognize and to realize that in the power of God we also, acting with God at our side, with Christ as our guide, with the Holy Spirit empowering us, are able to repair damages and are able to be reconciled with others.

Hope

We are not without hope. We are a people who can be God's agents for the reconciliation and redemption of this world, and we can start repairing the damages that we personally have caused and participated in. It is helpful to keep in mind Romans 8:31-39. "What then shall we say to these things? If God is for us, who can possibly be against us? He who did not spare his own Son but gave him up for us all, how will he not also fully give us all things? Who will bring a charge against God's elect? God is the one who justifies, who is the one who condemns? Christ Jesus is He who died, yes, who rather who was raised, who is at the right hand of God who intercedes for us? Who shall separate us from the love of Christ? Shall tribulation, or distress, persecution or famine or nakedness or peril or sword? Just as it is written, 'For thy sake we are being put to death all day long and were considered as sheep to be slaughtered.' In all these things we overwhelmingly conquer through him who loved us. For I am convinced that neither death, nor life, nor angels, nor principalities, nor things present, nor things to come, nor powers, nor height, nor depth, nor any other created thing shall be able to separate us from the love of God which is in Christ Jesus our Lord."

No estrangement, no sin, no wrong, no blindness, nothing in all of creation can separate us from the love of Christ. As you consider yourselves with honesty and openness, open your Bible to Romans 8:31-39 and keep it before you as a constant reminder that you are the beloved of God.

SPIRITUAL FRIENDSHIP

Step 8: Made a list of all persons we had harmed, and became willing to make amends to them all.

Discussion Topics

> Share experience of prayer time during past week.
> How has your attitude about others changed?
> Have you completed your list of persons harmed?
> Describe the experience of making the list? Was it painful? Shocking? Depressing?
>> Hopeful?
> What are your hopes and fears about making amends?

PRAYER TIME - STEP 8

Theme: Damages Done

STEP 8: Made a list of all the persons we had harmed, and became willing to make amends to them all.

Format

> Preparation (breath prayer, relaxation exercise, etc.)
> Read Psalm
> Silence (5 minutes)
> Read Scripture selection
> Silence (5 minutes)
> Personal prayers
> Lord's Prayer
> Collect of the week

Day 1:	Psalm 19	Ezekiel 18:21-23
2:	50	Matthew 6:14-15
3:	82	II Corinthians 2:7b-11
4:	85	II Corinthians 5:18-19
5:	118	I John 3:14b-20
6:	119:73-80	I John 2:9-11
7:	127	James 1:16-21

Collect

Almighty Father, who gave Your only Son to die for our sins and to rise for our justification: Give us grace so to put away the leaven of malice and wickedness, that we may always serve You in pureness of living and truth; through Jesus Christ Your Son our Lord, who lives and reigns with You and the Holy Spirit, one God, now and for ever. Amen.

Friday in Easter Week, (BCP, p. 224)

STEP 9:
Made direct amends to such people wherever possible except when to do so would injure them or others.

The 9th Step is intended to remove the divisions between us, to affect reconciliation where possible. Now we know that it is not possible under some circumstances to make amends; there are some things that we have to take to the grave with us. How do we determine where we can make amends, where we are being courageous, where we are being foolish and where we are being fearful?

VIRTUES NEEDED
Good Judgement
There are several virtues and qualities that we need for Step 9. The first is good judgment. Without good judgment we start doing things in an imprudent fashion, making apologies to people that are surprised in an unpleasant way or in ways that eventually lead to other problems. As you review your list from Step 8, begin to evaluate what the Lord would have you do. What is the Christian thing to do in each of those relationships? Good judgment is developed in part through the grace of God, in part by careful reflection upon who the people who are involved in our lives and from whom we are presently estranged or with whom we have some unfinished business. In part, and maybe even sometimes the biggest part, good judgment is developed by making mistakes and learning from them. That is where the careful review comes in. Where in your experience are quicksand, danger, or a mine field, dangerous property to tread upon; and where in your experience can you move through the mine field of possible danger to move towards reconciliation? Some reconciliations, of course, take practically nothing other than a simple apology; others take a great deal more effort. Determining which is which requires good judgment.

Good Sense of Timing
Once we have decided where we can move and how we can move, the next necessary quality is a good sense of timing. There are appropriate and inappropriate times to be reconciled. For instance, you don't want to attempt it during coffee hour at the church. That time is inappropriate not so much because other people would overhear, but because it does not give the other person any freedom in the relationship, so that you really sort of box people in. An apology made in public, even if the public is only one other person, prevents them from being able to respond freely, particularly if they are very angry with you and want to throw you out the window. You may want to keep company around just to prevent that, but in order to really be honest and to offer your own amendment; it does mean that we need to become open and vulnerable to the other person. Good timing is important there. If it is somebody whose personal circumstances are such at the moment that an attempt to reconcile would add to their troubles, then it needs to be delayed. You have to consider the other person, your own circumstances, and the circumstances of other people who are affected by any proposed amendment, apology, or reconciliation.

Courage
The third virtue necessary is courage. Courage is not fearlessness, but the willingness to take action in the face of great fear. When your legs are rubber and your stomach is in knots, it is walking into the situation seeking to be reconciled, seeking to be restored into fellowship with the other.

Prudence
Prudence is also important. God doesn't ask you to be idiots in being reconciled with one another. I

77

suppose there are those who would wish you severe harm. Certainly there are people who are so alien-ated from others that an attempt at reconciliation could result in a physical death.

Plan Your Approach

We have to be really clear about what we have done to injure other people and begin to make an evaluation of what an amendment will look like, what reconciliation will look like, and whether or not those amendments and reconciliation can occur without causing damage, or causing more damage, to the other person or to someone else. It is not fair, I think, to include yourself as one of the people who would get hurt. If you do that, you won't ever make reconciliation because it always hurts to say "I'm sorry" when you know you are dead wrong.

Priority One

Once you have reviewed each relationship, each strain, each brokenness, then begin the next Step of actually going out. Arrange your list by priority. You have to do something first, something second, and something third. Decide what those are by a sort of triage for your list. The first group of people would be those with whom complete reconciliation can be done right away. The offense was a minor thing, easily solved and you can deal with it all at one time and you can do it quickly. This is the immediate group.

Priority Two

In the second group are those where only partial amendment can be done because to fully disclose your wrong might create more damage for the other person. One of the situations that human beings get into, for instance, is sexual affairs. If you take the notorious triangle where Joe and Bob are best friends, and Joe was married to Mary. Bob and Mary had an affair with one another, but Joe never found out. However, due to other reasons, the friendship between Joe and Bob was broken. The reconciliation of that friendship does not include confession of the affair, if it is still unknown. That is one of those sins that can't be fully confessed. Perhaps Joe was unaware of his Mary's infidelity and for Bob, in attempting to restore his friendship with Joe, to cause a break in that relationship between Joe and Mary would be adding to the damage. So it has to be kept. You cannot create more damage in order to solve your own matters of conscience. If you do that, you create more conscience problems for yourself.

Perhaps you are cheating on expense accounts, how do you go about an amendment without losing your job? Perhaps if you have an understanding, very close employer, you might be able to say "I want to be able to repay it." But you might just have to understate your expenses on future vouchers in order to compensate for what was illicitly gotten earlier. That solves your conscience problem and restores the funds that had been wrongfully taken.

Another word about damaging others and some of the other concerns. First of all is the person that has been offended by us. Secondly, a loved one of that person, or family member, that would be injured by our apologies. Thirdly, our own family. For instance, somebody has been cheating on his expense account. There is a good chance, if he admits it to his employer he will lose his job and maybe go to jail. His family would be destitute if he did that. So his own family has to be considered. What is best for them? He should figure out a way to understate expenses as a way of repaying. One concern is your own family. Sometimes you may need permission from your family to take a Step because of the danger or the scandal that could ensue.

Priority Three

The third category of amendments would be those that need to be deferred until later. That is a situation where somebody has so much trouble in their lives that an attempt to reconcile would just create more trouble. Or perhaps they are in Europe and you cannot do anything about it right now. You have to wait for their return. Perhaps they are in the hospital, or sick, or on a trip—a variety of things can cause a need to defer. The principal consideration is that it is bad timing for the other person. Remember we are learning humility here, so we are placing ourselves behind other people's needs. While we may feel like we're busting to make an apology, sometimes it is better to just choke on it until a later time.

Priority Four

The last group is where amendment is not possible. Perhaps it is because you don't remember the name of the person that was offended, or you don't know where they are any more. There is nothing you can do to restore that. The broken relationship with a deceased grandparent or great-grandparent will have to wait until the Kingdom for repair. In this life it is not possible; although there is the exception mentioned in Step 8 where somebody who had felt badly about the way in which he had treated his grandparents went to their graves and at least said the words at the grave and felt some relief.

There are those where it is just not possible because you cannot locate the person, because they have died, because sometimes to broach the subject would create greater pain. To go back and intrude and try to make restitution is sometimes to bring up old wounds that have been successfully healed, and that creates an opening of an old wound and that is just not necessary.

As we consider making amends to people that we have injured, it is important to remember that we cannot buy peace of mind at the expense of other people. We have no right to cause more harm to other people in the name of justice, reconciliation and Jesus Christ.

Heal Small Hurts, Too

You may not even have any major fractures in your personal history. More than likely, what you usually have, if you have lived the normal, everyday, run-of-the-mill good life of trying your best day by day, are fairly minor strains and stresses. As you begin to change spiritually, to grow in the Lord, much of the amendment process has already begun. Some relationships begin to be healed where there was a little strain, or restored where there was a small break instead of a chasm. For instance, when you stop trying to control other people's lives, those relationships begin to be healed, because you are taking chains off. When you are trying to control somebody else's life, you have a leash around their neck, like a choke-chain. You jerk them back when they get out of line. You do it with your children in the name of good parenting. But we have to remember that what's appropriate for a five-year old by way of restrictions is inappropriate for a 16-year old. It is inappropriate for a five-year old to cross the street unaccompanied; it is inappropriate for a 16-year old to stay on the block and not cross the street. So, as you begin to let go of control, you find that amendment processes are already started.

The story is told about a wounded bird that a child takes and nurses back to health. He then has to let it go because it is a wild thing. He does not know whether the bird is going to return to him out of gratitude or affection or whatever birds feel, until he lets it go. So it is with our children, our spouses, our parents— we do not know for sure that somebody loves us until we let go of the controls on their lives. That is dangerous and risky business, because they may just leave. But unless we let them leave, there will always be an element of doubt. If you love something, set it free. If it doesn't return, it was never meant to be. If it does, love it forever. A lot of amendments begin when we set others free from our controls.

A lot of us, if not all of us, from time to time want to hold on to somebody more tightly than is appropriate. As we learn to trust God, and as we learn the serenity and comfort of trusting the Lord, then we also begin to learn to trust those other people with God, or to trust God with those other people. The

Lord will return to us the love that He wants us to have and will return it through the very people that we were trying to cling to. But now it is a voluntary love; it is a love that is real and true.

Change in Personality

It is not possible for us to really live a spiritual life, based upon spiritual principles such as these, without experiencing a real change in our personalities. We become less uptight, less possessive, less contentious. It may not happen overnight. It is slow nurture that helps us to grow spiritually, and that's what these spiritual principles are all about.

As relationships heal, as we change in our way of interacting with other people, we stop creating more broken and strained relationships. Until spiritual growth occurs serious amendment is futile, because new damages keep getting added to the pile.

It is important to remember at this point in the Quest that as a result of private confession (Steps 5, 6, and 7) all the debris of our life now belongs to God. It is not yours anymore, and so insofar as God is concerned, as you move forward from making a good clean confession, your offenses now are new first-time ones. It is a whole lot easier to turn around from a first-time offense than it is to tackle the mountain of the past. Private confession tackles the mountains and puts them in God's hands. Then when we do the same dumb thing all over again, we are not heaping it on that pile of stuff we left on the Lord's doorstep in confession, we are doing it for the first time. We can say, "Whoops, I don't think I want to do that" and we can then stop at the moment and make immediate amendment without it going further. We can say, "Gosh, I've been working on that one and I obviously haven't reached perfection yet. Let's back up five minutes and see if we can do this a little differently."

As you grow spiritually it becomes more and more frequent that you can stop when you have done or said something that you really wish you had not done or said, and say, "That was inappropriate, it was wrong of me to do it. I don't want to leave that sitting on the table here. Help me get around it and let's move on."

Live in Community

Spiritual growth always includes relationships with other people. We do not live in a vacuum; we are not islands unaffected by others. Part of our spirituality is to live in community. That is part of what the creation story is all about. Man is incomplete without woman—one human being is incomplete without another human being. We are meant to live in community, and what God does from the very beginning with Israel is to call a diverse people into community. What Jesus did when he started his ministry was to call twelve into community. At the end of his ministry he sent them out to make new communities. Judeo-Christian spirituality is strongly community-oriented. It is relational to other human beings. We are Christian humanists or we are nothing. You can be a humanist without being a Christian, but not the other way around.

Reactions

What can you expect out of people as you seek reconciliation with them? There are a variety of possible reactions, some of which will tie you up in knots. Some people will approve and praise you and say what a wonderful job you are doing. "It's really grand that you have owned up to this, and so I am going to let go of my animosity towards you. Let's embrace, let's be restored, and let's move on."

Others will condemn and reject any attempt at reconciliation. Now the danger to be avoided is getting drawn into an argument. Nobody has to accept anybody else's apology. If you are alienated from another person, you work through the review and decide this person is someone you can go to and attempt reconciliation. You want to do it, you believe God wants you to do it, and you choose a private place and a time when it is not going to create more damage as far as your judgment tells you. You go to the person and you say that you did wrong, that you regret it and that you wish to make restitution and to be restored to fellowship. They say, "Get the hell out! I never want to see you again! You did me wrong and I will never forgive that." Your initial reaction may be to blow up, "I came to you, I bared my soul to apologize, and you won't accept it?! Then you can go to hell!"

Humility needs to come into play. You need to be prepared for rejection, particularly when anything inside of you tells you that it might happen. There is an assertiveness training book called *When I Say No I Feel Guilty* in which are a number of listening skills. One, called "Fogging," is accepting the truth in somebody else's criticism—not the whole criticism, but the truth as you understand it. It is a good skill to have in your repertoire of things to say. When you are criticized, you can say, "Well, you're right, I was wrong and you don't have to forgive me." You have already admitted that you were wrong anyway. That is why you are there. So it is not really hard to think of saying that.

So be prepared spiritually and in your prayer life on the bigger ones where you could be rejected or attacked. God willing, you won't get blind-sided by one that you thought was going to be easy that turns out to be the hardest of all.

Principles Before Personalities

In amendment-making it is vitally important to practice principles before personalities. The issue that created the problems may not find resolution. The concern is not so much right and wrong, winners and losers.

Just because people disagree does not mean that either one is wrong. It also does not mean that either one is right. So often we fall into black and white thinking that says "This is my position and if you disagree with me, you must be wrong because I know I am right. Therefore, if there is a problem between us, it's your fault. I'm not willing to admit that I am wrong, so therefore you have to be." This attitude builds the wall higher and wider, like the Great Wall of China. Nobody defeated China by going over the Wall; they went around to the end and came in the back door. That is how you sometimes have to deal with broken relationships.

You have to give the other person the opportunity to accept or to reject you, but you do not have to take up a gauntlet when it is thrown down. You cannot control whether or not other people are going to accept or reject you or to start the argument over. What you can control, through the grace of God, is whether or not you argue with them. You can say, "I didn't come to argue those old points because I don't want to continue with a broken relationship. I want to seek common ground, a place where we can be in fellowship."

As we restore that fellowship, as we rebuild the foundation, and as the Lord leads us, perhaps somewhere down the line we can take up the tough issues again, more determined to listen, not only to each other, but for the Lord's will for us, which may be somewhere in between, or may not even be in the same ball park.

A Word of Caution

Be careful about saying there is nobody I can go to immediately and be careful about throwing everybody to the bottom of the list. Also be careful about removing people or situations from these bottom three (partial amendment, deferred amendment and impossible amendment). If in your good judgment, you place a situation or person down there, and you start making amendments and you find you are on a roll, that you are doing so well that you think you can handle the harder ones, submit that to prayer. If you still are convinced that you can handle them, go to your spiritual friend or your spiritual director, because your thinking could be muddied. When the Lord starts handling things for me, then I start thinking I can take over and do them. So be really careful about who is handling the work of reconciliation and get some help with discernment.

Restitution

Amendment frequently requires more than just admitting mistakes and apologizing. Restitution is also involved. If you take something that belongs to somebody else, and you say, "Gosh, I'm sorry I stole this watch from you," it is not enough. It takes removing the watch and giving it back—Restitution.

Penance

Sometimes it takes penance to complete the amendment. If it is something you cannot give back, then penance is required. A situation in youth ministry very recently was that a youth worker in a parish had been part of an unhappy party. He was the only adult present at a party; and he went out and bought beer for the minors. He couldn't take it back after the party was over; he couldn't make restitution, so penance became necessary. The penance for this young youth worker was one year of suspension of any contact with anybody under the age of 21 in any official capacity as a youth minister in the diocese. That is penance. He couldn't restore what had been taken away, and it wasn't okay. It took some time, some sanctions or restrictions.

Writing letters is not the best way to approach amendments, but sometimes it is the only way. Every once in awhile you read in the paper where someone has stolen $20 from a grocery store 25 years ago, and they finally are doing a house-cleaning. They write a letter to the store anonymously and say, "Twenty-five years ago I stole this money and this is what it is worth in compounded interest over the last 25 years. Here is $300." He never had a relationship with the store owner, but making restitution for wrongs done is important for the sake of conscience. If it is impossible to telephone or visit someone, then a letter is okay. Sometimes letters are the best way. Sometimes people read letters when they would not listen to you, would not open the door, or would hang up the phone. Having written it out and sent it, at least is an honest attempt at righting the wrong. If they still do not accept it, that is their business.

Change

The third thing that is necessary for real amendment besides restitution and penance is change. Saying "I am sorry that I took money out of your wallet" is not good enough if you're still in the wallet. If you don't intend to change, and you don't change, and you don't make any attempts to change, saying, "Gosh, I'm sorry that I don't let you watch what you want to watch on television and I always get my way," does not measure up unless you are willing to let the other person to have their way once in awhile and start to change. So change is the third element in real amendment.

Once we begin to change some amendment begins. When we decide to grow spiritually and to let the Lord change us, and when we do change, when our lives begin to change, then some relationships begin to heal and the amendment process begins. As healings begin, serious amendment becomes possible. Courage grows and danger lessens, so that eventually they meet.

SPIRITUAL FRIENDSHIP

STEP 9: Made direct amends to such people wherever possible, except when to do so would injure them or others.

Discussion Topics

Share experience of prayer time during past week.

Have you been able to make amends to anyone on your "list."

If not, why not? If so, what was it like?

How has your relationship with God been affected by the last few steps?

PRAYER TIME - STEP 9

Theme: Repairing the Damages

Step 9: Made direct amends to such people wherever possible, except when to do so would injure them or others.

Format

Preparation (breath prayer, relaxation exercise, etc.)
Read Psalm
Silence (5 minutes)
Read Scripture selection
Silence (5 minutes)
Journal entry
Personal prayers
Lord's Prayer
Collect of the week

Day 1:	Psalm 7	Matthew 5:23-25
2:	39	Luke 6:32-36
3:	69	Acts 20:32-35
4:	73	Romans 15:1-6
5:	119:25-32	I Corinthians 13:1-7
6:	123	Ephesians 4:25-32
7:	133	Matthew 18:23-33

Collect

O God, you have bound us together in a common life. Help us, in the midst of our struggles for justice and truth, to confront one another without hatred or bitterness, and to work together with mutual forbearance and respect; through Jesus Christ our Lord. Amen.

Prayer 28, *In Times of Conflict*, (BCP, p. 824)

STEP 10:

Continued to take personal inventory and when we are wrong, promptly admitted it.

Prompt, quick inventory tames our wrongs before they get a chance to grow into an ugly monster.

Daily Living

The last three Steps of the 12 are what I would call the "Daily Living Steps." They are the maintenance Steps, what we do on a daily basis. Step 10 is very important for keeping balance in life, to live to a good purpose under all conditions of good and bad alike. Some of the requirements for a continuous consistent high-quality spiritual life are to frequently and regularly look at both our assets and our liabilities, and to have a real desire to learn and to grow. It is like a balance sheet, looking at what we have that is coming in and what we have that is going out. We are trying to maximize the assets, and to minimize the liabilities.

What happens with folks, because of our Puritan heritage, 19th century Revivalism, and the moralism we have grown up with, is that we can look at our liabilities a lot quicker and more thoroughly than we can look at our assets. We really need to begin to learn to look at both, because as a matter of historical fact, most of us do a great deal of good in this world, probably more than we know. We have been told so many times not to get prideful, that if you say you are doing a good job then you are being prideful and you should not do that. We do not even look at a good job we do anymore. Of course, there's a scripture passage to back that up, "When you have done all that is required, say I have only my duty." You can take that to the extreme and get really sick and say "I haven't even done my duty." As we grow spiritually, and as we travel a spiritual journey, then we learn that we cannot live with excess baggage, we cannot live with emotional and spiritual hangovers. Anger, fear, anxiety, jealousy, hatred, prejudice, grudges, are excess baggage. Growth in Christ requires quick admission and quick correction of our errors so that we do not start filling up the bags that we cleaned out in Steps 4 through 9.

Out With the Bad, In With the Good

Remember the story our Lord tells about the demon being kicked out and the house swept clean. The demon goes and wanders and cannot find an abiding place. It comes back to the same old haunts again and finds your house swept clean and nothing there. So he gets seven more demons even uglier than himself to come back and fill the man's soul. As we sweep out the bad, we need to begin to fill it with the good, we need to keep the cobwebs knocked out of the corner and we need to keep the good stuff filling us. St. Paul says (Philippians 4:8) "All that is true, all that is noble, all that is just and pure, all that is lovable and gracious, whatever is excellent and admirable—fill all your thoughts with these things." Don't spend your time dwelling on the ugly in life. Look at the assets of life and the beautiful things in life and see what the Lord is doing well in your life.

When something enters your life that is not so good, deal with it quickly. Make an amendment rapidly and get rid of the dirty laundry or the skeletons in the closet before they have a chance to become a part of the clutter. A little cleaning every day is much easier than an annual spring cleaning.

When I was a prisoner of war, seven of us had been in the cell for about a week. We were never taken out of the place. Five of the guys had festering, infected wounds, and there was no medication to deal with it. That was one problem. The other problem was that we had the "honey-buckets" lined up by the door, and the guards did not allow us to empty them every day; and we never got to clean them out and scrub them. Those two items were part of our daily life, and we had been there with them as the odors had gradually worsened. One day at lunch time, the guard that brought the big pot of soup around came in, took one step inside the door and nearly gagged. He put the soup down, covered his face, and said, "Open the window, you need fresh air." We didn't know what he was talking about; we didn't smell anything, because we had been there while it was growing. But he wouldn't come inside the room. He took the soup outside and made us come outside and get it. About an hour later some guards showed up with automatic rifles. They opened the doors and the window and said, "Leave it alone" and left with the door of the cell open for about an hour and a half or two hours. Then the camp commander came around and gave us a lecture on personal hygiene. But he let it air out really well before he came around.

So with the ugliness in life, it will grow without you knowing it, unless you pay attention to it. In Hanoi, we did not have the ability either to clean the infected wounds or to empty the honey-buckets and scrub them out. But you have the ability to do your own personal spiritual house-cleaning. So do not deny yourself a clean house.

Time for Inventory

There are a variety of times and a variety of circumstances in which we can make inventory. Perhaps the best one is the spot check, becoming so consciously aware of your own spiritual growth and the ways in which you have changed and the ways in which you desire to change that when you do something that is troubling to you and to others you can stop right there and take a quick inventory and say, "Now what went wrong? This one snuck up on me. Let's see what it is." You will be able to name the demon, make an apology, an amendment and move on without it ever getting inside the door. The storms get calmed before they arise, and things get back into balance before they begin to teeter off to one side or the other.

That ability, which comes with growth and with practice, practice, practice, calls for a certain level of self-restraint in the face of both disappointment and personal pride. In the face of disappointment particularly, if we are the injured party, we must not become the victim. A victim is somebody who has no power. At this point in the Quest, we are beginning to regain some power; but now it is not our power, it is the Lord's power. In the face of personal pride, you can wrench your back patting yourself on the back. When you do something really good, be careful about going around and telling people how great that is. In school kids want to brag about the A's on their report card to their best friend and say, "Hey look, I got an A on that algebra test." What if his best friend got an F or a D? Bragging about the A could make the friend's pain worse.

Appropriateness

It is a good thing to be proud of success, but there is an appropriateness for sharing that success. Landing a new job is perhaps not the best thing to share with somebody who has just been laid off. The fact that you have a brand new healthy baby is not the best thing to share with somebody who has just had a miscarriage. Good judgment, timing, and sensitivity are important. Yes, you are joyful, you are filled with a sense of accomplishment, but you can hurt people even with that.

Honest Analysis

Daily inventory calls for honest and humble analysis. Review your actions and their results. Perhaps the results were unpleasant and your actions were faulty. Perhaps you really tried your best and things still turned out badly. The appropriate apology or amendment may be to acknowledge that you regret that things did not turn out well, or that you regret that you did the wrong thing.

There are many times when things turn out really well, but the efforts that you put into the situation cannot account for all the success. For instance, you can take a good deal of pride in landscaping your house, but you do not make the flowers bloom. That's up to God. And all the hard work and all the fertilizer and all the time and effort account for about 5% of what it takes to create a flowerbed. The other 95% is sunshine and rain at the right time, nutrients in the soil, and the fact that God created those plants in the first place. Honest analysis of our successes recognizes that "Yes, I participated in this success, and that's good. But I am not the only one. There were other people involved in it and God was heavily involved in it. I thank God that I had the privilege to be one of His co-creators and to share in making something beautiful of life."

Admit Faults

Regular inventory after honest analysis requires a willingness to admit our faults. Any human being is going to make mistakes. To live humbly, we need also to admit those mistakes. Honest inventory requires us also to forgive the faults of others, to forgive the humanity of another person. Without humble confession and forgiveness we begin to develop the twin ogres of hatred and grudges that will kill our spirituality. A grudge undealt with and unforgiven or a hatred will, like an enormous ugly cancer, grow and devour us spiritually. The only way to deal with it is to cut it out. Once you cut it out then it does not metastasize, it is gone.

Time Out

It is good to be able to do that right through the minutes of the day; but honestly, we sometimes get caught up in what we are doing and do not think about it and we miss the opportunity. So the next time for daily inventory is in the evening, before going to bed. Our Lord said "Don't let the sun go down on your anger." Sit down and take five or ten minutes and review the day from wake up call to right now. Pull out your appointment calendar if your have one, and look through it and say, "Now what happened today?" Take inventory. What was good that happened today? Thank God for that. What blessings were there today? Thank God for those. What mistakes were made, where was I disappointed by my own actions? Make your amendments. Where did I get caught up in an argument because I was not paying attention to what was going on? When we get caught in somebody else's arguments it is because we're not paying attention and we get blind-sided, hooked like a fish, we weren't looking at the hook, we were looking at the worm and we got the hook, too. If we are paying attention and somebody blasts us with criticism, then perhaps we can avoid an argument. If we have made a mistake, we can correct it; and if it is somebody else's garbage that they are dumping on us, then we don't have to accept it. We do not have to yell at them either. We can say, "Look, I don't think I am responsible for that one."

Plan Amendments

It is important as you write down both the good things that have happened and the mistakes that you have made, to plan amendments of wrongs for the next opportunity. If you have hurt somebody's feelings or said something unkind to somebody during the day, write a note to yourself that tomorrow you are going to make an apology.

Review Motives

As you look at the balance sheet, whether it is mentally or whether you have written it down, review your motives. Remember, motives are more important than the actions for our spiritual health. If you are kind to someone only in order to get something for yourself, then you have some amendment to make. Kindnesses can be sinful, too. You need to review motives and to develop honest regret, genuine gratitude, and a willingness to try again. The Episcopal Church has a baptismal vow to that effect: "Whenever you fall into sin, will you repent and return to the Lord?" That baptismal vow is a promise to try again, try again, try again.

The tools for spiritual house cleaning are a spot check during the day, the end of the day review, and a periodic private confession. Private confession is recommended at least annually. Lent is a good time; Good Friday is a particularly appropriate time; but also during Advent, and perhaps from time to time during the year if big things come up that are particularly disturbing. Even if your sins are just little stuff, annual confession is recommended just to sweep out the cobwebs from the corner in an annual or periodic review with a confessor.

Remember, inventories include both assets and liabilities. So when you are making inventory, do not forget to list your good intentions, your good thoughts, your good actions, and your good accomplishments, because there are plenty. With that on the left side of your yellow pad, the right side, the liability side, will not be quite so burdensome.

Make Room

One question that comes up in discussions of moral inventories is, "Isn't this terribly morbid? Why do we have to keep looking at our motives and reviewing all this?" It is not morbid, but it is difficult at first. It is like learning any new skill. It is hard work to develop a discipline of keeping a clean spiritual house. Our purpose is to make room for the love of God and the fellowship of God's people.

If your motive is to feel bad about yourself and to condemn yourself for being a terrible sinner, you have missed the point of the Spiritual Quest. The total depravity of humanity is a sick notion that came out of the right wing of the Calvinist movement. If you want to feel just horrible, there are those who think you should. There have been monastic movements in history where self-flagellation was part of the spiritual discipline. If you had a wicked thought, you beat yourself with a leather strap. There is that sort of strand of morbidity that for centuries has been present within certain circles of Christian thought.

Accentuate the Positive

The Spiritual Quest, these 12 principles of spiritual growth, is focused on the positive. The reason we are looking for negative stuff is to eliminate them so we can grow positively. The emphasis is on the virtues and the development of virtues; such chivalrous notions as courtesy, kindness, justice, and love—things that you find in the Bible, that Jesus talked about. That is our focus.

Debris that you just leave lying in the background sometimes grows big and trips you up. It is best to get those things out where you can see them. Satchel Paige once said "Don't ever look over your shoulder because something might be gaining on you." But it is important in spiritual growth to periodically take a look around at your own spiritual household and take inventory. Offer everything to the Lord and let Him give back to you what is good for you.

Like the little boy in the "Bloom County" comic strip, knowing you have an anxiety closet is bad enough; but the idea of having to be locked in it with those anxieties is more than some of us can handle. Remember that we are talking about spiritual progress here, to grow, to progress, to learn. Perfection is not a goal. None of us are going to reach perfection in this life. Do not worry about perfection. Focus on progress. Remember, learning from mistakes and failures is progress. Making them may not be very pleasant, but not learning from them is to slide backwards. If we learn from our mistakes and failures, then we progress.

Fertilizer or Garbage?

It is the mistakes, the failures, the troubled times that are probably the richest resources for learning most about ourselves, our Lord, and about other people. In reviewing the bad times in life, say, "What can we learn?" That is how we live into the Biblical phrase that says "All things work together for good for those who trust in the Lord." Notice it doesn't say that all things that happen are good. It says all things work together for good. There is a lot of bad stuff that happens in life. Everybody knows that if they are honest. In looking at these bad things, by analyzing and praying over them, then we can learn. As we learn, we grow; and as we grow, we progress *toward* perfection.

There is a general thanksgiving on page 836 in the Book of Common Prayer that addresses this balanced approach to the moral life:

"Accept, O Lord, our thanks and praise for all that you have done for us. We thank you for the splendor of the whole creation, for the beauty of this world, and for the wonder of life, and for the mystery of love. "We thank you for the blessing of family and friends, and for the loving care which surrounds us on every side. We thank you for setting us at tasks which demand our best efforts, and for leading us to accomplishments which satisfy and delight us. We thank you also for those disappointments and failures that lead us to acknowledge our dependence on you alone.

"Above all, we thank you for your Son Jesus Christ; for the truth of His Word and the example of His life; for His steadfast obedience, by which He overcame temptation; for His dying, through which He overcame death; and for His rising to life again, in which we are raised to the life of your Kingdom.

"Grant us the gift of your Spirit, that we may know Christ and make Him known; and through Him, at all times and in all places, may give thanks to You in all things. Amen."

SPIRITUAL FRIENDSHIP
STEP 10: Continued to take personal inventory and when we were wrong promptly admitted it.

Discussion Topics
Share experience of prayer time during past week.
What has been your experience of journal keeping for the past two weeks?
Have you been able to make quick amends during the past week?
Name three insights into God you have gained during the Quest.
Discuss your spiritual reading.

SELF-AFFIRMATION

Divine order takes charge of my life today and every day. All things work together for good for me today. This is a new and wonderful day for me. There will never be another day like this one. I am divinely guided all day long, and whatever I do prospers. Divine love surrounds me, enfolds me and enwraps me, and I go forth in peace. Throughout today my life is calm, centered and focused.

Whenever a stressful experience upsets me, I immediately return to a peaceful, joyful existence. At all times I am aware of the abundance of God, whose basic love for me makes fear, anxiety or worry useless activities and emotions.

I am a spiritual and mental magnet, attracting to myself all things which bless and prosper me and others. I am a wonderful success in all my undertakings today. I choose happiness all day long. Throughout today I am in constant gratitude to God for the rich way he continues to bless me.

From Clergy Stress, by Roy M. Oswald
© Ministers Life Resources, 1982
Copied with permission from Ministers Life, Minneapolis, MN 55416

PRAYER TIME - STEP 10

Theme: Vigilant Review and Repair

Step 10: Continued to take personal inventory and when we were wrong promptly admitted it.

Format
    Preparation (breath prayer, relaxation exercise, etc.)
    Read Psalm
    Silence (5 minutes)
    Read Scripture selection
    Silence (5 minutes)
    Journal entry
    Personal prayers
    Lord's Prayer
    Collect of the week

Day 1:	Psalm 40	Matthew 7:9-14
2:	41	Matthew 11:28-30
3:	53	Matthew 18:21-22
4:	62	Acts 3:19-20
5:	101	I Corinthians 10:12-13
6:	119:57-64	I Corinthians 13:11-13
7:	138	Romans 8:10-13

Collect
    Set us free, O God, from the bondage of our sins, and give us the liberty of that abundant life which You have made known to us in Your Son our Savior Jesus Christ; who lives and reigns with You, in the unity of the Holy Spirit, one God, now and for ever. Amen.

Fifth Sunday After the Epiphany, (BCP, p. 216)

STEP 11:

Sought through prayer and meditation to improve our conscious contact with God as we understood him, praying only for knowledge of his will for us and the power to carry that out.

We have come full circle from that first Step when we admitted we were powerless over sin. In Step 11 we are praying to God for the power to carry out his will in our lives.

Essential Elements
Regular Prayer

There are three very essential elements for developing this conscious contact with God: Regular personal private prayer is the first one. Every day since the beginning of this course, you have been urged to set aside ten or fifteen minutes to spend with the Lord. You have managed that with varying success, although nobody has been perfect at it, even if you have kept the daily schedule. You continue to grow and you continue to use your time with the Lord better.

Safe and Honest Environment

The second essential element for developing a conscious contact with God is a safe and honest environment for verbalizing the experience of God. That is what the spiritual friendship is all about. Spiritual life is probably more private and intimate in most people's minds than their sex life. People are more willing to talk about their sexual behavior than they are about their prayer behavior. That is not to say, "Ain't it awful." It is to say that this is so important to us that we sometimes guard it very, very strongly and sometimes find ourselves unable to share verbally with another person. Part of the Spiritual Quest has been to develop a safe and honest friendship. There are all kinds of safe friendships which are non-challenging, that do not confront us when we are in error and do not hold us responsible for doing what we promised to do. Those safe relationships are not honest ones. Honesty includes confrontation, accountability, and support. Supporting one another in our journeys is to hold each other accountable. I am not going to hold you accountable for MY spiritual development, but I will hold you accountable for your own. That is what the friendships are.

Corporate Worship

The third essential element for developing a conscious contact with God is regular, frequent corporate worship. That is why we begin every session with worship as an integral part of what we do together. It is also why Lord's Day Eucharist is stressed so strongly, because it is receiving the Body and Blood of Christ. We also receive the Holy Spirit as we participate in the community of faith in an open and expectant fashion, expecting the Holy Spirit to work in our lives and in our parish and in our worship.

So those three things—regular, personal, private prayer; safe, honest environment for verbalizing the experience of God; and regular, frequent receiving of Holy Communion—are essential elements in developing intimate, conscious contact with God.

Goal of Prayer

The goal of prayer suggested by Step 11 is <u>not</u> to get our way, <u>not</u> to be healed, <u>not</u> to have perfect relationships. The goal of prayer is very simply *union with God*: To know we are one with God; to know that the Lord loves us and lives with us and we live in Him. That union, that conscious contact with God is as necessary for a full and complete life as are air, light, food, clothing, and shelter. To be a completely full human being requires a spiritual aspect in life. The spiritual aspect begins to permeate all the rest of life and to fill the rest of what it is we do in life, so that everything that we do becomes infused by the spirit of God.

Without prayer, our souls become undernourished and we wither and die. Like a person undernourished from the nutrients that sustain the body, the soul first becomes bloated, like the little tummies of the children who are starving to death, and it appears to be full; but so many souls are starving to death for the love of God. They appear to be full, but if you touch, you can feel the tightness is different and there is a sickness that is tragic. The sickness is a result of poor prayer or no prayer.

Kinds of Prayer
Self-examination
Through the last seven Steps we have talked about and experienced self-examination, meditation, and other kinds of praying. Self-examination is like a farmer tilling the soil, breaking it up, letting the nutrients get free and providing the environment in which new things can grow. The no-till method of farming does not work well spiritually. You can't just cast your seed on hard ground and expect anything to happen. The birds will come and eat it up or carry it away. Spiritual soil has to be tilled. Self-examination breaks the hard crust, gets rid of the rocks, gets rid of the weeds, gets rid of the extraneous matter, in order that new seed may grow.

Meditation
The kind of prayer in which we listen for God is meditation. Meditation is converting the nutrients in the soil and in the young plant to life, enabling the spiritual photosynthesis which is a natural God-given part of what it is to be human, to be enlivened and to draw the health from the soil and to draw into ourselves those things which cause us to grow in Christ.

Intercession
Prayers of intercession and prayers for guidance are the things that enable that young plant of ours, that young soul of ours, to begin to grow branches so that we can reach out to the world. As our Lord told the parable of the mustard seed, it is such a tiny little thing when it is first sown. But when it is fully grown, it is large enough so that small animals can find shelter underneath and the birds of the air can find a place to roost. So it is with our souls; we may be insignificant when we get started, the Steps may seem terribly difficult, or the idea of the ability to be a spiritual leader, a recognized spiritual person in the community, seems so far fetched; but if we will be patient with ourselves, if we will nurture that small seed, and plant it in good soil, and provide the nourishment and the food and the sunshine, then slowly that seed will break lose and start shooting down roots and start shooting up branches. As we continue to soak in sunshine from the leaves and nutrients from the roots, then the branches begin to appear and then the shade. The analogy the Lord used about the mustard seed is a good one here as we think about how we grow.

Other Varieties
There are varieties of prayer. The traditional list is probably pretty well known: Adoration, thanksgiving, confession, intercession, petition, praise. We adore God just because He is God, praise Him for the wonders He has performed, and thank Him for the goodness He has given us. Confession is telling Him what we have done wrong. Intercession is prayer for others; petitions are prayers for ourselves. The Prayer Book is full of them. In the Eucharistic Rite we have all kinds of prayers. The *Gloria in excelsis* is a hymn of praise. The collect of the day is typically a prayer of petition. The prayers of the people are

intercessions for the Universal Church, its members and its mission, for the nation and all in authority, for the welfare of the world, for the concerns of the local community, for those who suffer and for those who are in any trouble, and finally for the departed. As the church gathered prays for those things, so it is good for us in our individual, private prayers to remember that we are connected with all those categories and all those subjects for intercessory prayer and to include them in our daily prayers.

In God everything is present. God is infinite. The psalms say "A thousand years in your sight is like a day when it is passed, and a day is like a thousand years." Day and night, years and centuries, are governed for our purposes by the rotation of this planet and its orbit about our sun. When you get out in the cosmos, our days are irrelevant. When we talk about astronauts spending three days in space, they have been around the earth many, many times. They have seen day and night come and go before they get tired. With God it is even more so. In God's time there are no barriers of death or time.

The invocation of the saints is like me asking you to pray for me, because in God's time we are all present. That is why we pray for the departed, because perfection in the Kingdom of God is not static. Clarence Jordan, a Baptist preacher down in south Georgia, said in a sermon one time that his idea of heaven had nothing to do with pearly gates and golden streets. His idea of the Kingdom of God and heaven was that he would be able to do for eternity the things that gave him the most satisfaction on this earth. His greatest satisfaction came from winning souls to Christ. So his idea of heaven was to be sent by the Lord to those who were dead but were still separated from God. He tells the story about Joe and the train. Joe was a man who hadn't given his life to Christ, but one day he was thinking about it really hard. He was thinking about it so hard that he didn't hear the train, and BAM, the train got him. Jordan said, "Now I ask you, is Jesus more powerful than a locomotive? Can you picture Jesus saying, 'Oh shucks, I almost had him. If he just had paid attention, he would have missed that train and he would have given his life to me, but, gosh, that's the breaks—to hell.'" Jordan said "That's absurd; Jesus is more powerful than a locomotive." His idea of heaven would be to get up to the pearly gates and Jesus would say, "Hey, Clarence, I got a problem. You remember Joe? Ever since that incident with the train, he hasn't been speaking to me at all. Do you think you could go over there and do something with him?" He said "That's my idea of heaven, to be able to go over and win somebody for Christ."

C.S. Lewis was another one who said he thought heaven and hell were exactly the same place; it's just that your perspective was different. People in hell were people who lived in heaven but didn't know it, like the dwarfs in the *Last Battle* of the *Chronicles of Narnia*. He also told the story of the man being shown around hell. All the people were sitting around a table set with an abundance of the most delicious food. Unfortunately, they all had splints on their elbows, and were unable to feed themselves. So they were condemned to being at a banquet forever out of their reach. He was then shown around heaven. The scene was exactly the same, but instead of being miserable, the people were feeding the person across the table from them.

In the Prayer Book

In the Book of Common Prayer, pages 810, 811 and 812 is a table of contents of Prayers and Thanksgivings. They are divided into prayers for the world, the church, national life, the social order, the natural order, family and personal life, and some other prayers for use in the evening, before and after worship, before and after receiving communion, grace at meals, and that sort of thing. Then come about 11 thanksgivings, a couple of general ones and then some specific ones for church life, national life, social order, natural order and family and personal life. There are some wonderful prayers in there. Some go back to the first English prayer book, some to the first American prayer book. The prayer of St. Francis is in there.

Printed Prayers Enable Us to Pray

So that is a source for prayers, to teach us to pray. The prayers in the Prayer Book are not prayers; they are words on a printed page. They will do you no good if you keep the book on your coffee table or put it under your pillow and try to get it by osmosis. They don't become prayers, like scripture doesn't become scripture, until you ingest it, until you make them your own. Some of these written prayers, if you will use them on a regular basis, will become yours, and then they will be real prayers. Sometimes in prayer we find that we are unable to speak, unable to verbalize our deepest yearnings because there are some things that just defy words.

As you become familiar with written prayers, when you are in a situation and words fail you, you can open a Prayer Book and find the prayer that fits. It may be in the back, it may be in the front in the collects, it may be in the prayers for Morning or Evening Prayer. The more familiar you are with the Prayer Book, the more you will learn to pray.

Praying in Public

Most of us get absolutely uptight when we even suspect that somebody might ask us to pray out loud in public. Dave Barks, a Presbyterian minister who did some tapes some years ago, was a student at the Presbyterian seminary on Lookout Mountain. A friend of his came to Chattanooga and they were having dinner in the Choo Choo. They were sitting in the restaurant, the two of them at the table, and the meal was served. His friend just sat there, and Barks was not sure what to do, if he expected to say grace or not, and he didn't want to bring it up. His friend noticed his discomfort, and said, "David, would you like to say grace?" David said, "Yes, I really would." So his friend took a knife and rapped on his glass, ding-ding-ding-ding-ding, and said, "Hey, everybody, the Rev. Mr. Dave Barks would like to return thanks for this meal." At that point, the only thing Dave could think of to say was "Our Father, who art in heaven..." Then he tried to kick his friend, who had very strategically placed his legs behind the front legs of his chair, so that he kicked the chair instead and hurt his foot.

When you know you are to be called on to pray in public, prepare for it. You get a microphone, people, a football stadium full of folks, that is no time to go blank. So always prepare. A good Prayer Book will help you. Almost everything in the Book of Common Prayer is a prayer. The Psalter is Israel's prayer book and hymnal. Many of them ask God's protection, many of them are hymns of praise. The psalms are a good source for prayer.

Hymns Are Prayers

The other source for prayers is a good hymnal. Most hymnals have seasonal divisions, Holy Days, Holy Communion, Marriage, Holy Trinity, Praise to God, to Jesus Christ, to the Holy Spirit, the Church, the Church's Mission, Christian Vocation. They are poetry, songs and prayers. It was St. Augustine who said, "He who sings his prayers, prays twice."

Poetry will paint pictures in your mind that simple prose cannot do, although some prose writers are very poetic. Archbishop Cranmer was one, C.S. Lewis was one, various fantasy writers particularly are poetic prose writers. Sometimes the 1611 Bible is good for poetry too; I don't understand it very well anymore because I have gotten used to reading modern English.

Those are sources for prayer, to help us to continue through prayer and meditation to improve our conscious contact with God. Effective communication is not just sitting in your chair for fifteen minutes in quiet meditation. It is not just saying two or three prayers and stumbling through a few petitions or a prayer list. You also communicate with God when you sing, in your poetry, in the psalms, through other prayers that other people have written that you find beneficial in your lives. All of that is included. All of it helps to open us up and broaden us out so that the love of the Lord can come in, and union with God can become a reality.

We say in this Step that we're praying for knowledge of God's will for us and the power to carry that out. Now how in the world are you going to know when you know what God's will is? That's the issue. Anybody who says, "I know what God's will is" should be given a wide berth. Remember that Satan has always been a seducer, and likes to quote scripture. He quoted scriptures to Jesus to get Jesus to disobey the Father. Satan said, "It's God's will that You be filled and so turn these stones into bread. God doesn't want You to suffer out here in the wilderness." He said, "God's will is that You would be the king of the earth, so You can have that today All You have to do is worship me and You will fulfill God's will. It's God will that everybody should follow You, so all You have to do is jump off the pinnacle of the temple and He will send his angels to lift You up and everybody will know that You are the Son of God. And God's will will be fulfilled." Those were the temptations. So, be careful.

How do you know? Well, the best thing to use to be absolutely certain about God's will is hindsight. It is looking back and reviewing. That is why it is a good idea to keep a journal, so you can look back and see where you were in your Spiritual Journey.

History is important in discerning God's will for the present. As we read the history of the scriptures, world history, history of the church, and our own personal histories, we begin to see over and above the petty arguments of our times the overarching will of God, working his purpose out to usher in and establish a kingdom of love on this earth. Sometimes it is really obscure because of the horrible things that are happening in the world like the plagues of the Middle Ages, the world wars of the last century, the internecine warfare that the church has been engaged in since the Reformation, the fights over prayer book revision, the ordination of women, or whatever else we're fighting over. We also look closely at people who say that they know what God's will is, and we discover that they are wrong. We know they are because the results of their actions are destructive. As Jesus said in the Sermon on the Mount, "Beware of false prophets, men who come to you dressed up as sheep while underneath they are savage wolves. You will recognize them by the fruits they bear." (Matthew 7:15-16)

Like chemical addiction, religious addiction is a real problem in our world today. Through addictive black and white thinking, people are condemned to hell because of the way they believe, the way they interpret the Bible, or the way they worship. Since God sent his son into the world not to condemn, but to save, we can be pretty sure that the condemnatory person is not speaking God's will.

Sometimes you see somebody who is really a pretty decent person, whose efforts are well intentioned, but whose results are disastrous. Since Jesus came to bring life abundant, we can be pretty sure that disasters are not his will.

A priest who was assigned in his first parish in Gulfport, Mississippi, humorously said, "Jesus wants me to be on the beach." Well, if he had been serious, that would be either an unconscious or a blatantly conscious rationalization about where he was going. It would be nice to think so, but it's not it. Our wishful thinking about our lives frequently distorts the divine guidance that we claim for ourselves. Jesus said we must leave all else behind, take up our cross, and follow Him.

A husband or a wife who says "It is God's will that I leave my family and go off to the missionary land and never come home again" is distorted. But they will quote the scripture to you ("You have to leave father and mother, and husband and wife and children for the sake of My name.") to rationalize their abandonment of their Christian vows, their vows before God, to their spouse and children.

A problem we may have is that we do not know enough about the Bible to know whether they are quoting in context or out of context, or if they're quoting Dante or Shakespeare or Will Rogers. We do not have a counter-scripture to challenge them. During the stewardship time of the year, everybody's favorite verse is, "Don't let your left hand know what your right hand is doing." That is to say "Don't ever sign a pledge card." But Jesus also said, "Let your light so shine before men that they may see your good works and glorify your father which is in heaven." It depends on what you want to do as to what you're going to quote.

What so many of us do in claiming the Lord's will is to decide what we are going to do and then figure out how we can justify it scripturally. That is a problem. We know that, and if we are sensitive Christian people, we are very wary in our own selves of claiming to know God's will. It leaves us walking somewhat in a fog. There is an Argus poster that has a fog-enshrouded path leading into the woods, and the inscription on it is something like, "Lord, I do not need to see the whole way but just enough to know the next step." That is the kind of humility that goes along with truly seeking the Lord's will.

Sometimes in our search for the "power to carry out" the Lord's will, we are like Jesus was in the Garden of Gethsemane on Maundy Thursday night. We sweat bullets over what is going on and then say, "Lord, I don't want to do this, but let Your will be done, whatever that is" or "Lord, I DO want to do this, nevertheless Your will be done." As we live into Step 11, we need to have "Your will be done" as an intentional and honest part of our prayers, particularly when it comes to petition or intercession.

In 1972 there was a student in seminary who had a brain tumor. There was a group of seminarians who prayed with him daily that he would be healed; and they were confident that the Lord would heal him. He died. They were devastated, because their intention was that the tumor go away and that he be left in this life. They did not see that dying was part of God's healing and their faith was shattered. Some of them left seminary.

When we are in opposition to God's will, a clue is that there is internal agitation, a struggling with God. Another clue would be an overwhelming desire to control. A third one would be a sense of being off-balance, like the whole thing was fixing to fall apart, or we are going to come unglued or fly apart.

Taking time out to say "Thy will be done" often opens a channel that is otherwise choked up with anger, fear, frustration, and misunderstanding. When you find yourself with those clues going off, exploding within you, it is time to say, "Look, let's take a five minute time out and pray about this, settle down and come back later."

One thing to be absolutely avoided is any notion that you know what God's will is for other people. "Lord, the church needs some martyrs. Those people over there would do just fine." Much is to be gained about knowing God's will, and this is a final word on this, from reviewing history. If God has a purpose in mind with this created order, that purpose is probably still on track and He probably has not changed it much. So review history, scriptures, tradition, church history, and look at your own experience in the past. Then you can begin to really get a better idea of God's will.

SPIRITUAL FRIENDSHIP

STEP 11: Sought through prayer and meditation to improve our conscious contact with God through Our Lord Jesus Christ, praying only for knowledge of His will for us and the power to carry that out.

Discussion Topics

Share experience of prayer time during past week.

What personal changes have you made or plan to make in your prayer discipline?

How does your spiritual reading effect your conscious contact with God?

How does your servant ministry and stewardship effect your conscious contact with God?

Has Journal keeping been helpful?

THE COMPLETE DAILY OFFICE

MORNING PRAYER

Seasonal Opening Sentence	p. 75-78
Confession	p. 79
Invitatory and Psalter	
Seasonal Antiphon	p. 80-82
Venite (Su, Tu, Th, Sa)	p. 82
Jubilate (M, W, F)	p. 82
Christ our Passover (Easter)	p. 83
Psalm (Daily Lectionary)	p. 934-1001
The Lessons	
Daily Lectionary	p. 934-1001
Old Testament	
Canticle (as appointed)	p. 144
Epistle	
Canticle (as appointed)	p. 144
The Apostles' Creed	p. 96
The Prayers	
The Lord's Prayer	p. 97
Suffrages A (M, W, F)	p. 97
Suffrages B (Su, Tu, Th, Sa)	p. 98
Daily Collect	p. 98-100
Prayer for Mission	
"Almighty..." (Su, Th)	p. 100
"O God..." (M, W, Sa)	p. 100
"Lord..." (Tu, F)	p. 101
Other Prayers & Thanksgivings	p. 814-841

	Sunday	Prayers 1, 7, 18, 27, 44, 45, 54, 69
		Thanksgivings 3, 10
	Monday	Prayers 2, 8, 16, 19, 29, 35, 41, 46, 48, 54, 56, 57
		Thanksgivings 4
	Tuesday	Prayers 3, 9, 20, 30, 39, 42, 47, 54, 58
		Thanksgivings 5, 10
	Wednesday	Prayers 4, 10, 21, 31, 36, 44, 46, 49, 54, 59
		Thanksgivings 6
	Thursday	Prayers 5, 11, 23, 33, 37, 40, 52, 54, 60
		Thanksgivings 7, 10
	Friday	Prayers 6, 14, 25, 32, 41, 46, 53, 54, 61
		Thanksgivings 8
	Saturday	Prayers 17, 26, 34, 38, 40, 54, 55, 62
		Thanksgivings 10
	General Thanksgiving	(Su, Tu, Th, Sa) p. 101
		(M, W, F) p. 836
	Prayer of St. Chrysostom	p. 102

EVENING PRAYER

PRAYER TIME - STEP 11

Theme: Growing in the Lord

Step 11: Sought through prayer and meditation to improve our conscious contact with God through Our Lord Jesus Christ, praying only for knowledge of his will for us and the power to carry that out.

Format

    Preparation (breath prayer, relaxation exercise, etc.)
    Read Psalm
    Silence (5 minutes)
    Read Scripture selection
    Silence (5 minutes)
    Journal entry
    Personal prayers
    Lord's Prayer
    Collect of the week

Day 1:	Psalm 63:1-7	Luke 11:1-10
2:	143	Romans 8:15-18
3:	4	Mark 12:28-34
4:	8	Luke 12:22-31
5:	15	II Corinthians 12:7-10
6:	19	Ephesians 5:6-17
7:	57	Philippians 4:5-8

Collect

    Grant to us, Lord, we pray, the spirit to think and do always those things that are right, that we, who cannot exist without You, may by You be enabled to live according to Your will; through Jesus Christ our Lord, who lives and reigns with You and the Holy Spirit, one God, for ever and ever. Amen.

Proper 14, (BCP, p. 232)

STEP 12:

Having had a spiritual awakening as the result of these steps, we tried to carry this message to others, and to practice these principles in all our affairs.

We are at the last of the Steps in the Spiritual Quest, although in reality there are no last Steps. We take these Steps over and again, particularly the last three, the "daily living steps" of daily evaluation, of daily effort to increase our conscious contact with God and to pray for the knowledge of His will for us and to pray for the power to carry out His will for us. This 12th Step begins with an uplifted hope ("Having had a spiritual awakening as a result of these Steps") followed by the "evangelistic" Step "to carry this message to others and to practice these principles (the 12 Steps) in all of our affairs."

Joy

Step 12 is a joyous step. It is a bubbling up and over kind of thing, having come alive. So many people walk around apparently alive. They eat and breath, their hearts beat, they get up every morning, go to work every day; but they are not really alive.

There is a movie called *The Music Box* about a guy whose job is to put tops on one-gallon containers of windshield washer fluid. He stands at a conveyor belt with other people, and they just screw the tops on. Everybody is living dead. They go to work, but they are dead. The awakening comes for him when he is on his way home through a dismal, snowy street and a group of angels stop him. You know they are angels because they are in white tuxedos and have little wings. He does not know what they are, but we do. They tell him the story of the King and sing this alleluia song. He gets all excited about it; but he is the only one who is excited, so he tries to hide it. He has come alive, but he has not quite figured out what to do with it. The angels leave him a music box, which he hides under his coat. He goes home playing it and realizes it is shocking to his wife and annoying to his son. So he shuts it up and goes to the bathroom to play it, as though they cannot hear it. But his wife and son can hear it, but he is not sharing it. Finally, one night while he is asleep the angels come back to the bedroom and wake him up by clearing their throats politely. He tries to shush them. He says, "She wouldn't understand." But they say, "The gift is to be shared." He protests, so they start singing the song. Of course, she wakes up, and the angels are dancing around the room. She understands completely. The son comes in and joins in the dance and everyone comes alive. He finally realizes that this is something to be shared.

Share the Good News

The prophets talk about the word of God burning within them unless they speak. Cleophas and his companion on the Emmaeus Road, when they realize who it was that was with them, say, "Did not our hearts burn within us." They did not know it was Jesus, but now they can look back and say, "We weren't fully aware." They thought they were aware, but like the man in the movie thought the world was "just that way" until life suddenly and radically changed for him when he became aware of Christ in his life. Then it just bubbles out.

Converts are just that way. People go off to Cursillo, come back enthusiastic and they want to share with everybody, and it gets right obnoxious. They just bubble all over themselves. Those of us who are still back home half asleep do not care to be wakened up that rudely. So we consider it irritating. But you just cannot help yourself when you are filled with the love of God. There is a great deal of joy that comes from a spiritual awakening, but you cannot manufacture the thing. That is what the Step says. It does not say, "Having developed a spiritual awakening" or "Having created one for ourselves" but rather "Having had one." It suggests that the awakening is a gift to us from God. The Steps enable us to place ourselves more closely in the presence of God and to attune our spirits to God's will and to risk the vulnerability and openness that allows God to enter into our lives. Then the awakening occurs.

That is what happens to many people who go to Cursillo, or Happening, or Faith Alive, or other spiritually-oriented retreats. They are open just a little a crack because some friend of theirs said "It won't hurt. It'll be good for you." They open a little crack, and in the course of the event, they begin to trust the other people there and then allow the door to be opened further. When they come back they are enthusiastic.

Be in God

Remember, "enthusiasm" means being "in God" in Greek (en Theo). They come back filled with God. It has been rather disconcerting for us Episcopalians, who do not go in for all that stuff. Loud, noisy alarm clocks are not very pleasant. But sometimes the only way to wake some people up is with a stick of dynamite.

As a teenager I slept through a fire alarm in our apartment house. My mother woke me up about half way. I went in the bathroom and got dressed because I thought it was time for school. I looked out the window and it was dark. I came out and finally heard the fire alarm going off. I never heard it earlier. Another time I was in camp in North Carolina where they played "Nothing could be finer than to be in Carolina in the morning." I always tried to get up before that thing came on, so I could have a little preparation time. So sometimes it takes a lot to wake people up from a deep slumber. Other times, a little chirping sound will do it, or a cheerful word from someone who is already awake, or a beam of sunlight coming through the window and warming your face.

The spiritual awakening comes as we begin to rouse ourselves and to help God to rouse us from our slumber. That is what those first 11 Steps are all about. It is their thorough practice that prepares us for the gift of the first half of the 12th Step—the Spiritual Awakening.

A Review
Step 1

By way of review, the 1st Step is when we admit that we are unable to control sin in our lives; we are unable to control evil in the world, and we are powerless over it. Nobody wants to be powerless over anything, but we are indeed powerless over sin and evil. It is going to creep in, even when we are vigilant.

Step 2

Step 2 moves from the sense that we cannot control the wickedness in the cosmos, sin and evil in our lives, to the understanding that God can restore us to rationality. There is a problem with telling people that, because their image of God is not very helpful. It is the stern criminal court judge. The Bible pictures God as a judge, but most usually it is a civil court judge, like Solomon deciding who was mother of the baby. The criminal court judge is the person who is going to send you to jail. He is going to find you guilty and send you to jail. The civil court judge is the one who discerns the truth about something. He finds that which is good, wholesome, and redeemable and brings it out.

One of the problems we have been having in our country in recent years has to do with the inadequacy of the English language to fully express the religious experience. It is the same inadequacy Paul found with Greek when he tries to describe his "out of the body" experience, and when he tries to describe the love of Christ for the church as similar to a husband-wife relationship. He winds up by saying "It's a mystery. It wasn't a really great explanation, but it's the best I could come up with given the confines of language."

Another problem in our culture today has been the male image in Scripture relative to God. In recent years, the awareness of the damage done by fathers to their children has come to the surface of everybody's consciousness. There is a lot of negativity about the imagery of "father." If you are trying to talk to somebody who has never much been around the Church, who is not aware of the good side, and all they know is a miserable, drunken jerk of an abusive father, and you call God your "father" then the only content they have to fill the word "father" is that abusiveness. That is not really helpful for God. That is difficult to deal with in our Scriptures. There are ways to deal with it without saying that Jesus was androgynous (having both sexes), but we need to explore other images that are less filled with garbage from people's history.

If we don't know somebody's history and we talk about our experience of God, then we may be proclaiming a very negative Gospel. Church membership can mean joyful things to some people and absolutely miserable things to others. It can mean the place where acceptance is found; it can mean the place where the nun beats you over the knuckles with a ruler if you use your left hand, or if you get out of line. It can be where the mean people, boring services, and long sermons are. We have to remember that the word that we proclaim is what is *heard*, and not what is *said*. We may know exactly what we mean because of all the background we have, and we make a lot of assumptions about what people understand and know. If they do not have that background, then they will take our words, fill them with their background, and the result may be 180 degrees out of phase with ours. They will be hearing a story that is not intended to be said.

However, it is entirely possible to be sensitive to other people. In the proclamation of the Gospel it is really important to do what Paul did in Athens, that is, go in first and learn something about the people you want to talk to, and get to know them. "Be a friend, make a friend, and bring a friend to Christ." You have to be a friend first; then you can make that person your friend and bring him or her to Christ. You offer yourself; you find out about the other person so that they can begin to offer to you. Then you can speak about the Gospel in terms they can hear.

The rationality that we find as we trust God restores us to wholeness, to sanity. Being a whole human being includes being a rational being, using our brains, our intellect to its fullness, not checking it when we come in the front door of the Church. A lot of folks in our Christian tradition are not allowed to ask questions, because "you don't question God." You don't ask the "why" questions, like "Why did a 12-year-old get run over in front of his house?" or "Why did a 16-year-old die of cancer." "It is God's will" is supposed to settle the question. That is not rational and is not a satisfying answer. A more rational answer would be "I don't know. God knows, but he is not telling right now." A rational response is "God suffered the loss of a son, too. It was a terrible tragedy, but in the death of that Son, new life was brought and, as dreary and dismal and horrible as life was, it began to turn around three days later, and the world has been changed. Maybe there is some redemption in the deaths of children, or the tragic deaths of loved ones. There is no definitive answer." I think it is more satisfying to say that. It leaves open the possibility of search and more pursuit of knowledge, understanding, and the will of God than just clamping it off with "It's God's will. Accept it and forget it." The world is full of people who have been told growing up "God said it. I believe it. That settles it." But that is not rational.

Step 3

What we discover in the process of the Quest is that rationality is something that God gives us and will give to us if we will take the 3rd Step and trust God to care for our wills and our lives, not to take us over and operate us like a marionette, but to care for us. Caring for us includes sending us out of the house. Caring for our children means that at some point in their maturity we allow them to cross the street by themselves. We cut the protective covering we gave when they were helpless. We stood back when they attempted those first Steps, knowing they were going to fall down. When they learned to ride bicycles and drive cars and whatever they have done in their pursuits in life, we began to cut off our protection as a way of caring. Of course, when they get into trouble, the way we care for people is to let them accept the consequences of their willful actions rather than going out and rescuing them and getting the judge to "fix the ticket."

God cares for us in similar ways. If we want to be stupid, he lets us be stupid. If we want to go off and leave the church from 18 to 24, he says, "Go ahead and do it. It's a dumb thing to do, but go ahead. I'll be waiting for you like the father waited for the prodigal son. When you get back we'll have a party." That is part of the caring. We don't develop our wills and our lives without skinning our knees. God knows that and lets us skin our knees; but He is there to doctor them when we do, just like mom and dad did when we were little kids.

Step 4

In Step 4, having made that decision to turn our wills and our lives over to the care of God, we discovered we needed to find out what those wills and lives are. So we searched around to identify exactly what is there—good, bad, and indifferent.

Steps 5-9

Once we found it, it was time to do something about it. The garbage needed to be cleaned out and taken to the dump. That is what the 5th Step is all about. The good stuff needs to be sorted out, rearranged, polished up, and put back into use. Those Steps begin to give God a better shot at doing something with our wills and our lives by getting rid of the debris. We identify the debris and give it to God to carry it off. As we sort through, we become willing to let God do it; we ask Him to remove our flaws. Once we have done that, we say, "Since we don't live in isolation, since we live in community, where have we done damage to the community?" Step 4 had to do with how we had damaged ourselves. Step 8 has to do with how we have damaged those around us. We search out those damages; then we go and repair them where we can.

Steps 10-12

Then we begin the daily living Steps after we have, with the aid of God, straightened things up. Daily we examine our lives and review what we have done and immediately make amendment when we have goofed up. When we snap at somebody that didn't deserve it, we stop and say, "I'm sorry." We make our apology and repair the damage done before it has time to fester like an infected wound.

We then continue to seek God's love and will for us through prayer and meditation, through participation in ministries of outreach and putting ourselves in places where God works both in our private prayer places, in our public prayer places, in our action places of outreach. Somewhere along the line, God willing, the Holy Spirit moves us and we wake up from the doldrums and we have sometimes a radical, quick conversion, and sometimes a more slowly growing transformation in the way in which we look at life, the way in which we do things, the way we feel about things. Sometimes it takes a lot of hard work.

They May Be Simple, But They're Not Easy

People who are in 12 Step recovery programs find it is hard work. It takes a long time, with a lot of relapses into the old ways of doing things, old behavior patterns, old way of thinking. It then takes a real struggle to move back out of them. Sometimes the spiritual awakening is like the person who is just exhausted and is having to be awakened in slow stages. Sometimes it is like St. Paul on the Damascus road, when the alarm clock goes off and suddenly we are awake, up, alert, and ready to go. When we are fairly well refreshed when we go to bed and have a good night's sleep and wake up refreshed and ready to start the new day. We don't always do that. Sometimes we are ill; sometimes we have worked hard the day before or played hard or we don't sleep well at night. Then it is harder to get up in the morning. Spiritual life is like that.

A New Power

We find that nothing we did on our own could ever produce those results. This is different from when we were working without God and trying to rely on our personal resources. Now we have a power under-girding us that enables us to rejuvenate and to come alive more quickly and easily and gloriously. Then a greater sense of direction is found in life. Maybe we don't change anything about our careers, or our lifestyle, but they suddenly become filled with the joy that we always hoped would be there. Sometimes the Lord leads us to a different way of living.

Transfiguration

One image that is really helpful here is "transfiguration" as opposed to "transformation." These Steps do not transform us from the devil's people to God's people. Transfiguration was when Jesus was shown to Peter, James and John to be what he always was: the fulfillment of the law and the prophets. As the pre-existent, co-eternal Logos of God, he was always the fulfillment of God's purposes, always the Word of God. Peter, James and John got a vision of that on the Mount of Transfiguration when they woke up from a deep sleep and looked up and saw Jesus with Moses and Elijah. This is descriptive of what happens to us. We wake up and begin to recognize ourselves as the beloved children of God, not a little brat who is in trouble with daddy. We think of God less and less in terms of the "jailer" or the "angry parent" who is really perturbed with our sinfulness, and more and more in terms of a father or mother who, when the child goes astray, reaches out and brings them in and helps them to repair, dries their tears, mends their skinned knees, props them up on the bicycle, and helps them to totter off again. The child feels safe with that parent. He is not afraid because the bicycle got wrecked and the fenders got scratched. The father is concerned that the person not be injured and tries to heal the person.

Tuned In to God

Sometimes we find that we are turned from danger as we trust God. Intuitive awareness comes to us as we attune ourselves to the will of God. We get the sense that we need to go tend to somebody, or avoid some danger. In the midst of our daily routine we say, "I have to stop this because someone is in need." And we go. So we become more aware that we are now instruments of God and we are moving out, following the lead of God.

On December 18, 1972, my mother-in-law had a dream in which I came into her room holding my helmet under my arm. She asked why I wasn't wearing it. That was the night I was shot down. I don't understand it, but she was a very spiritual person, aware that God was working in her life, and communicating with her in her dreams about real life matters of concern.

If we are attuning our lives to the will of God, then naturally there are a lot of qualities that will begin to grow in us, like honesty, tolerance, selflessness, peace of mind, serenity, love. All of them are gifts of the Spirit, love being the principal gift and the one which Paul admonishes us to seek above all else. Nothing else is worth anything unless you have love. In I Corinthians 13 he elaborates on it. With love, honesty makes sense, and tolerance means something, and selflessness is no longer being a lapdog. You can be selfless out of love without being somebody's doormat, whereas if you don't love, you can be selfless and do good for people constantly, but find that you're a sick co-dependent rather than a healthy loving person. Good action and bad action often look alike; it's often the motive behind it that determines whether it is good or bad.

It's A Gift

The spiritual awakening is a gift from God. The only way to keep the gifts from God is to give them away. The only way the man could keep the music in *The Music Box* was to open it and share it with others around him. He found out that when he let the music out of the box, his enjoyment of it was not diminished just because other people heard and enjoyed it. Everyone was able to receive full measure without any diminishment whatsoever because it was shared.

An important characteristic about giving is that it can be wonderful or disastrous depending upon our motive and their content to the words we use. You cannot attach strings to your giving. If you are sharing the love of God on the condition that people appreciate what you say, on the condition that they be converted, or on the condition that they come to church with you, those are strings that make prisoners.

Evangelism Is Its Own Reward.

Sharing the love of Christ is it's own reward. Remember the saying of Jesus that "Some people pray on street corners *in order to be heard by others*. I tell you, they have received their reward." They got heard by men. Big deal. That's it. There is no further benefit, and not much change in others lives or ours. Don't demand anything from the recipient of whatever it is you are giving in the name of Christ. If Christ leads you to give a gift to someone else, figure Christ has his own motives and your ego probably is not one of them.

Sharing the benefits of the spiritual life is its own reward, too, because it will strengthen you. If you talk nice about somebody, you will develop a good attitude towards the person you talk about. If you talk ugly about somebody, you will develop a bad attitude towards them and a sense of guilt in their presence and estrangement in the relationship. So say good things. That is what Peter said to do in his letter, to talk well of others. William Porcher DuBose, an American Episcopal theologian, was dean of the seminary at Sewanee at the turn of the century. He was confronted one time by someone who said, "I have read your books, and only one time have you ever even mentioned Satan." DuBose is reported to have said, "Well, I hope I spoke kindly of him." That is the attitude we need, to speak well of people.

Kindness Returns

Jesus said, "Be good to those who persecute you, and thereby heap coals of fire upon their heads." It is not to burn them to the ground; it's the cauterizing fire that seals off their wounds and converts them to a friend. Be kind to your captors, your enemies, and convert them to friends. If you fight them, they will fight you back. That was really clear to me in Vietnam when I was alone and surrounded. It is not so clear to teenagers in school, especially when they are suffering from "testosterone poisoning," having to flex their muscles to show how manly they are. It is not too clear to them that they can turn the other cheek and be kind to one another. God willing, they will put away childish ways after they pass the peak of hormonal production at age seventeen, and start cooling off after that. Then they will learn that kindness and gentleness is not necessarily wimpishness.

If we do good to others, we become stronger, too. If we think kindly of others, if we fill our heads with kindly thoughts, we won't have a lot of room for anxiety or animosity or other unpleasantries that would perhaps otherwise fill our thoughts.

The Harvest Is In God's Hands

Paul says "Apollos planted, I watered, and somebody else will reap the harvest. God gives the growth." Don't be too anxious or compulsive or worrisome about what is going to happen if you share an experience of God with another person. Let that be a seed-planting exercise. Let God do in their life what He will and let it grow. There are times when those planted seeds take years and years before they ever break through the hard crust of somebody's life and you can see them begin to sprout up. Stories are told about people writing to their Sunday school teachers of thirty years ago and saying, "I wanted to tell you that you meant so much to me, and that what you said to me as a child really meant a lot." The teacher may wonder "What did I say?" Perhaps those who return to the church after a time away do so because of the seed planted in their childhood by a kind elder.

Looks Are Deceiving

Deciduous trees look dead in the winter, but they are not. They are growing stronger. People are like deciduous trees. Around age 18, many people depart from the church. John Westerhoff describes that faith struggle moving from the "faith of our fathers" to owned faith where it is transformed from a "coat" to your "skin." It takes some time to do that. Some people have to shed everything in order to find out what is good. It is a kind of extended 4th Step for the person in the "searching faith" time of life when they throw everything off thinking that the faith of their parents is just old junk. Then as they realize they have to have something, they go back and rummage through the cast offs and find out what is worthwhile for them.

Love Begins At Home

Much of what we do by way of evangelism is within the household of faith. There are a lot of people who yearn to hear the word of God, a kindly word, who are faithful members of the Church. We know that and respond well when someone is ill or hospitalized or has a death in the family. But it is also true at other times. One of our callings in the Church is to become more attuned to how we can speak the loving word of God within the parish.

Grief, for instance, doesn't go away right after the funeral. Even after some healing is evident, significant anniversaries (birthdays, weddings, the death of a loved one, holidays) continue to be occasions of pain. A widowed person can quickly become very lonely. Having dedicated every waking moment for years, perhaps, to the benefit of a sick spouse, they are desperate to hear of the love of God spoken through the voice of one of God's Christian people. I received a phone call from a man widowed some months earlier after caring for his home-bound wife for five years. He started out by asking, "How long does this last?" During the five years of his exclusive care of his wife, he had been gradually separated from all his friends and outside interests. He had a really difficult readjustment, and there was a real need for the Christian community to respond to him to assist with the process by showing the love of God.

Evangelism is one beggar telling another beggar where the bread is. That beggar can be a faithful Christian or somebody who has never known Christ. Everyone you know is an appropriate subject for your witness. Jesus said, "Freely you have received, freely give." That is the watchword for us in this Step.

Not Just Sunday Morning

This Step calls for us to practice these principles in all of our affairs. That is the point stressed in the Quest all along. The spiritual life is not just something we do in our private prayers or public worship. You have been encouraged to take on a ministry of outreach, to be part of both worship and fellowship activities of the church, and to engage in other kinds of ministries in your families and among your friends. We do not live before God alone. We live before God, yes, but we also live in community. We are seeking to be Christians 24 hours a day, seven days a week without any letdown. That is the goal.

Progress, Not Perfection

Having said that, I must hasten to remind you that we are talking about spiritual *progress* and not spiritual *perfection*. If you have not found perfection after 14 weeks, don't worry about it. Give yourself a break. But if you haven't found *progress* after 14 weeks, then go back to Step 1, get all the handouts, and work your way through the *Spiritual Quest* a little more seriously.

The 12 Steps are progressive and make sense when combined one after the other in the order in which they are presented. It takes all of them. They are sequential, make sense, and are beneficial when practiced in order. Jumping from Step 1 to Step 12 is not going to get you very far.

You cannot be an effective witness if you are holding in, covering up something in your life, and only offering a little piece. Being an effective Christian witness means the willingness to be vulnerable to others and to be a kind of window on God. Let people see how God works in your life, including how God works in your life when you are being obstinate. The Bible is full of examples of how obstinate people are instruments of God. Jews and Christians kept those stories because they give us all hope. So let people see your life as fully as you can. They will see more than you wish they would, anyway.

Joe-Harry Window

There was a pair of psychologists who developed the image of a four-paned window to describe how people see us. One window is transparent: you know some things about yourself that everyone else also knows. One window is one-way out: you know what is there, but no one else can see in. Another is one way in: you do not know something about yourself that everyone else does. The fourth window is opaque: it is your dark side. Getting the dark window smaller through prayer and mediation is a goal. Making all of the windows more transparent is also a goal—not so people can rummage through our dirty laundry, but so they can see God by looking at us.

Am I My Brother's Keeper?

Remember, too, you *are* your brothers' and sisters' keeper. When Cain asked God the question, "Am I my brother's keeper?" The answer was, "Of course you are, you dolt, and you killed him." In the baptismal promises, and in all the rites of transition, we are asked, "Will you do all in your power to support this person in their Christian journey?" And we promise "Yes, we will." Being our brother's and sister's keeper in Christ is to support each other in our resolve, to hold us accountable for our decisions and our actions, and to prod us on the way in the spiritual journey. When one of us is sinking in the mud, then those of us who are on solid ground support by reaching out and bringing them to safety. When somebody is drowning, someone has to jump in and drag them out, sometimes at the risk of our own lives. We are each others keepers in Christ. Spiritual Friendship begins to open the idea up.

Mother Teresa of Calcutta said, "Christ has no body now on earth but yours, no hands but yours, no feet but yours. Yours are the eyes through which Christ's compassion looks out on the world. Yours are the feet with which he is to go about doing good. And yours are the hands with which to bless us now." The Lord works through you and me. I encourage you to take the opportunity. Consider how you can be emboldened to share Christ with another, and how you can approach someone who seems to be asleep at the switch. Wake them in ways in which they can be receptive to the Gospel that you bear. If it means dynamiting their chair in order to wake them up, maybe you have to do that. If it means a kiss on the cheek, like Prince Charming and Sleeping Beauty, then do that. Know your source of strength; know your subject; proclaim the Source in ways that the other person can understand and receive the love of Christ.

SPIRITUAL FRIENDSHIP

STEP 12: Having had a spiritual awakening as the result of these Steps, we tried to carry this message to others, and to practice these principles in all our affairs.

Discussion Topics

How has your spiritual awareness changed in the last three months?

How have you taken the Good News of God in Christ to others?

How has your use of the Steps effected the way you relate to other people?

Do you want to continue the Friendship relationship with your Quest partner? If so, when will you get together?

Would you like to continue the group meeting for study? Prayer? Worship?

PRAYER TIME - STEP 12

Theme: Evangelism in Word and Deed

Step 12: Having had a spiritual awakening as a result of these steps, we tried to carry this message to others, and to practice these principles in all our affairs.

Format

Preparation (breath prayer, relaxation exercise, etc.)
Read Psalm
Silence (5 minutes)
Read Scripture selection
Silence (5 minutes)
Journal entry
Personal prayers
Lord's Prayer
Collect of the week

Day 1:	Psalm 16	Matthew 25:31-40
2:	45	Luke 10:25-37
3:	46	John 13:31-35
4:	66	John 15:11-17
5:	99	Romans 5:1-5
6:	119:65-72	Galatians 5:26-6:10
7:	145	Romans 10:11-15

Collect

Almighty God, You have poured upon us the new light of Your incarnate Word: Grant that this light, enkindled in our hearts, may shine forth in our lives; through Jesus Christ our Lord, who lives and reigns with You, in the unity of the Holy Spirit, one God, now and for ever. Amen.

First Sunday after Christmas Day, (BCP, p. 213)

BIBLIOGRAPHY

Arndt, Johan. *True Christianity*. New York: Paulist Press, 1978.

Athanasius. *The Life of Antony and the Letter to Marcellinus*. New York: Paulist Press, 1980.

Boehme, Jacob. *The Way to Christ*. New York: Paulist Press, 1978.

Bonaventure. *The Soul's Journey Into God, The Tree of Life, The Life of St. Francis*. New York: Paulist Press, 1978.

Edwards, Tilden. *Spiritual Friend*. New York: Paulist Press, 1980.

Foster, Richard J. *Celebration of Discipline*. San Francisco: Harper & Row, 1978.

Foster, Richard J. *Challenge of the Disciplined Life*. San Francisco: Harper & Row, 1985.

Foster, Richard J. *Freedom of Simplicity*. San Francisco: Harper & Row, 1981.

Fowler, James W. *Becoming Adult, Becoming Christian: Adult Development and Christian Faith*. San Francisco: Harper & Row, 1984.

Fowler, James W. *Stages of Faith*. San Francisco: Harper & Row, 1982.

Greene, Thomas H. *Weeds Among the Wheat*. Notre Dame: Ave Maria Press, 1984

Gregory of Nyssa. *The Life of Moses*. New York: Paulist Press, 1978.

Holmes, Urban T., III. *A History of Christian Spirituality*. New York: Seabury Press, 1980.

Holmes, Urban T., III. *Spirituality for Ministry*. New York: Harper & Row, 1982.

Hosmer, Rachel and Jones, Alan. *Living in the Spirit*. New York: Seabury Press, 1979.

Jones, Alan. *Exploring Spiritual Direction: An Essay on Christian Friendship*. New York: Seabury Press, 1982.

Jones, Alan. *Journey into Christ*. New York: Seabury Press, 1977.

Jones, Alan. *Soul Making: The Desert Way of Spirituality*. San Francisco: Harper & Row, 1985.

Julian of Norwich. *Showings*. New York: Paulist Press, 1978.

King, Martin Luther, Jr. *Strength to Love*. New York: Collins, 1977.

Law, William. *A Serious Call to a Devout and Holy Life, The Spirit of Love.*
New York: Paulist Press, 1978.

Leech, Kenneth. *Soul Friend: The Practice of Christian Spirituality.*
San Francisco: Harper & Row, 1977.

LeGuin, Ursula. *The Earthsea Trilogy.* New York: Bantam Books, 1975.

Lewis, C. S. *The Great Divorce.* New York: The Macmillan Company, 1952.

Lewis, C. S. *The Chronicles of Narnia.* New York: The Macmillan Company, 1956.

Lewis, C. S. *The Peralandra Trilogy.* London: John Lane, 1946.

Lewis, C. S. *Till We Have Faces; A Myth Retold.* New York: Harcourt, Brace, 1957.

Link, Mark. *YOU: Prayer for Beginners and Those Who Have Forgotten How.*
Niles, IL: Argus Communications, 1976.

Luther, Martin. *The Theologica Germanica.* New York: Paulist Press, 1980.

Moltmann-Wendel, Elisabeth. *The Women Around Jesus.* New York: Crossroads, 1982.

Nouwen, Henri. *Reaching Out: The Three Movements of the Spiritual Life.*
Garden City, New York: Doubleday, 1975.

Nouwen, Henri. *Wounded Healer: Ministry in a Contemporary Society.* Garden City, New York:
Doubleday, 1977.

O'Connor, Elisabeth. *Journey Inward, Journey Outward.* New York: Harper & Row, 1968.

Pennington, M. Basil. *Centering Prayer: Renewing an Ancient Christian
Prayer Form.* Garden City, New York: Doubleday, 1980.

Richard of St. Victor. *The Book of Patriarchs, The Mystical Ark, Selections.*
New York: Paulist Press, 1978.

Saliers, Don E. *Worship and Spirituality.* Philadelphia: The Westminster Press, 1984.

Sanford, Agnes Mary. *Sealed Orders.* Plainfield, New York: Logos International, 1972.

Sheehan, John F. X. *On Becoming Whole in Christ.* Chicago, Loyola University Press, 1978.

Simeon the New Theologian. *The Discourses.* New York: Paulist Press, 1980.

Smith, Martin. *Reconciliation*. Cambridge: Cowley Press, 1986.

Smith, Martin. *The Word is Very Near You: A Guide to Praying with Scripture.* Cambridge: Cowley Press, 1989.

Teresa of Avila. *The Interior Castle*. New York: Paulist Press, 1979.

Thornton, Martin. *English Spirituality.* London: SPCK, 1963.

Weil, Simone. *A Gateway to God*. New York: Crossroads, 1982.

Weil, Simone. *Waiting for God*. New York: Harper & Row, 1951.